The Rajah-Moonje Pact

Documents on
A Forgotten Chapter of Indian History

Edited by
Devendra Swarup & Meenakshi Jain

Originals
Delhi-110052

ISBN 978-81-8454-078-9

Published by
Originals
(an imprint of Low Price Publications)
A-6, Nimri Commercial Centre,
Near Ashok Vihar Phase-IV,
Delhi-110052
Phones: 27302453
e-mail: info@lppindia.com
visit us at: www.lppindia.com

Printed at
D K Fine Art Press P Ltd.
Delhi-110052

PRINTED IN INDIA

Contents

Introduction

In 1932, in the wake of the second Round Table Conference, two pacts were concluded in quick succession between leaders of caste Hindus and the Depressed Classes. Both were intended to counter colonial ploys to wrench the Depressed Classes from Hindu society and thereby stymie the nationalist upsurge. While the Poona Pact, associated with Mahatma Gandhi and Dr. B.R. Ambedkar, acquired a landmark status in modern Indian history, the earlier Rajah-Moonje Pact, espousing identical principles, has been all but eclipsed in popular memory.

This is somewhat perplexing, given that the British themselves had then grasped the import of the accord between M.C. Rajah, President of the All India Depressed Classes Association, and B.S. Moonje of the Hindu Mahasabha. Though maintaining official silence, they closely monitored the fallout of the Pact. One indicator of their concern was the file maintained on the Pact in the Government of India Reforms Office (N.A.I.: File No. 111/32-R). Its very title, "*Representation of Depressed Classes in the future Legislature — Issue of joint vs. separate electorates — Raja-Moonje Pact*," bears witness to British awareness of the significance of the accord.

Curiously, in a departure from routine practice, no duplicate was made of this file which opens with the Secretary of State,

Sir Samuel Hoare's, telegram of 1 March 1932 to the Viceroy asking for details of the Pact and the level of support it enjoyed. Immediately following are several pages of typed and handwritten correspondence of senior British officials on the matter. Why British officialdom chose not to follow the norm of preparing printed copies of this file remains inexplicable. Suffice it to note that the file contains the original copies of several important documents. Were it to disintegrate or be damaged in any way the documents would be lost forever.

The file additionally contains memorandums and letters submitted by Depressed Class leaders to high-ranking British authorities in the wake of the Round Table Conferences in London. Also appended are over fourty pages of clippings from leading English language newspapers on events related to the Pact, testimony to the wide coverage it received.

Announced in February 1932 amidst a raging controversy on the appropriate means of ensuring representation to the Depressed Classes in the provincial legislatures, the Rajah-Moonje Pact was the first ever agreement on reservations and a joint electorate between caste Hindus and the Depressed Classes. In its outright rejection of separate electorates then advocated by the British and Dr. Ambedkar, it was a blow to divisive colonial politics and Ambedkar's assertions to Depressed Class leadership.

By then M.C. Rajah's seniority and credentials as a Depressed Class leader had been well established. In 1916, over a year before Ambedkar's return to India on completion of his studies abroad, Rajah had been appointed secretary of the Adi-Dravida Mahajan Sabha in Madras Presidency. In 1917, he had negotiated a pact with Dr. T.M. Nair of the Justice Party, to safeguard the interests of the Depressed Classes in the Presidency. Rajah was the first Depressed Class leader to be nominated to the Madras Legislative Council in 1920. In 1922, he had successfully moved a resolution in the legislature that the name "Pariah" be dropped in favour of "Adi-Dravida" and "Adi-Andhra" in the Tamil and Telugu districts respectively. In 1927, Rajah was nominated to the Indian Legislative Assembly, the first Depressed Class leader to be so honoured. He had been elected President of the All India Depressed Classes Association in 1928 when Ambedkar was invited to serve as Vice-President. Rajah's *"The Oppressed Hindus,"* published in 1925, was the first work in English by a member of the Depressed Classes.

Why Rajah should have chosen to enter into an agreement with B.S. Moonje rather than Gandhi, then the undisputed leader, is unclear. One reason perhaps could be the inaccessibility of the Mahatma who was imprisoned immediately on his return from the Round Table Conference. Gandhi's known opposition to the principle of reservations on caste lines could have been another inhibiting factor. It is also possible that Moonje, who had led a Hindu Mahasabha delegation to the Round Table Conference, was projected a Hindu leader and hence may have seemed an appropriate choice to Rajah. Some press reports claimed that the initiative for the accord had come from Moonje himself (*The Statesman* 9-4-1932). Be that as it may, despite the stir it created, the Rajah-Moonje Pact was superseded six months later by the Poona Pact, which reiterated the agreement on reservations for the Depressed Classes with a joint electorate.

Politics of numbers

The events surrounding the Rajah-Moonje Pact spotlighted the conflicting approaches to the problem of the Depressed Classes throughout colonial rule. The British, preoccupied with the political dimension, were from the time of the first decennial census in 1871-72, "obsessed" with the question whether Untouchables could properly be classified as Hindus (Mendelsohn and Vicziany 1998: 27-29). Though no specific guidelines were issued during the 1881, 1891 and 1901 census operations, Census Superintendents like Denzil Ibbetson made efforts to collect data on selected castes and tribes. In 1901, the Census Commissioner of India, H. H. Risley, introduced the principle of social precedence for the classification of castes. At the time of the 1911 Census clear instructions were given to officials, "to enumerate the castes and tribes returned or classed as Hindus who do not conform to certain (religious) standards or are subject to certain disabilities." The reference was undoubtedly to the untouchables (Gupta 1985: 36-40).

By then, attempts to de-link the Depressed Classes from Hindu society were considerably under way. A memorandum presented to Lord Minto in 1906 by a deputation of Muslims, and drafted as per the suggestions of his private secretary (Hardy 1972:156-157), had argued that, "The Mahommedans of India number, according to the census taken in the year 1901 ...between one-fifth and one-fourth of the total population of His Majesty's Indian Dominions, and if a reduction be made for the uncivilized portions of the community enumerated under the heads of animist and other minor religions, as well as for those classes who are ordinarily classified as Hindus but properly speaking are not Hindus at all, the proportion of Mahommedans to the Hindu majority becomes much larger" (Gopal 1964: 330).

Dr. Ambedkar himself commented on Muslim attempts to use the Depressed Classes to reduce the numerical strength of Hindus. "The Muslims," he said, "have always been looking at the Depressed Classes with a sense of longing and much of the jealously between Hindus and Muslims arises out of the fear of the latter that the former might become stronger by assimilating the Depressed Classes. In 1909 the Muslims took the bold step of suggesting that the Depressed Classes should not be enrolled as Hindus" (Ambedkar 1946: 235).

The declaration on 20 August 1917, on the goal of British policy in India, gave a fillip to the politics of numbers. Lala

Lajpat Rai observed that after the announcement "a great political capital" was made of the Depressed Classes and their number arbitrarily increased (Rai 1928: 100). "In 1917", he stated "...the total population classed according to the list in the *Quinquennial Education Report* as depressed amounted to around 31 million persons...Since then the number has swollen, and in the report of 1921 itself the total figures mount up to nearly 52.7 millions... But the Census Commissioner *guesses* that the number may be between 55 and 60 millions" (Rai 1928: 96-97).

The British did not stray from their course in subsequent years. In 1932, when the issue of Depressed Class representation had created a crisis, Sir Frederick Sykes, Governor of Bombay Presidency, reaffirmed the long-term British policy to draw the Depressed Classes into the political process and thence separate them from Hindu society. In a letter to the Viceroy, Lord Willingdon, on 7 June 1932, he stated, "I consider that for political purposes the depressed classes should be considered as a community distinct from the Hindus and their representation should be treated as a subtraction from the Hindu vote"[1] (Shourie 1998: 233).

Social reality

The social reality was, however, at variance with colonial requirements. The untouchables were local, at best, regional groups unconnected with one another. In an attempt to artificially transform them into an all-India community, the British, around 1901, floated the term "Depressed Classes" which was picked up by English educated caste Hindu reformers, who found it less repugnant than the term "untouchables." Depressed Class leaders, however, described the term as "degrading and unacceptable." Ambedkar suggested "non-caste Hindus," "protestant Hindus," "excluded castes," "non-conformist Hindus" and "exterior castes" as alternatives. He himself preferred the last term because "it defines exactly the position of the untouchables who are within the Hindu religion but outside the Hindu society…" (Gupta 1985: 32). The All India Depressed Classes Association recommended the term "Adi- Hindu."

Besides lack of unanimity on nomenclature, there was also uncertainty about the groups to be included in the category of Depressed Classes. A resolution moved in the Imperial Legislative Council in 1916 by M.B. Dadabhoy on measures to ameliorate the conditions of the Depressed Classes raised the question of the criteria to be adopted for determining backwardness. Rai Sahib Babu Rama Charana, member of the United Provinces Franchise Committee, observed that the tenor of discussions in the Imperial Legislative Council implied that the Depressed Classes included criminal and wandering tribes, aboriginal tribes and untouchables (Gupta 1985: 8-9).

Efforts to identify depressed groups proved inconclusive. The Director of the Census of India for 1921 observed, " It has been usual in recent years to speak of certain sections of the community as the 'Depressed Classes.' So far as I am aware the term has no final definition, nor is it certain exactly whom it covers" (Gupta 1985: 11).

A meeting of the Superintendents of Census Operations in January 1931, on the eve of the decennial exercise, noted that, "No specific definition of depressed castes was framed and no more precise instructions were issued to the Superintendents of Census Operations, because it was realized that conditions varied so much from province to province and from district to district, even, within some provinces, that it would be unwise to tie down the Superintendents of Census Operations with too meticulous instructions" (Gupta 1985: 15).

A questionnaire distributed by C. H. Lothian, Chairman of the Indian Franchise Committee in 1932 asked, "What communities would you include as belonging to depressed classes? Would you include classes other than untouchables, if so which?"(Gupta 1985:16). M.G. Hallett, Secretary to the Government of India, in a telegram to the Viceroy on 21-8-1932, also admitted that "the depressed classes have not yet been defined and…possibly in some provinces there will be no such cases" (N.A.I.: File 31/113/32-Poll and unprinted K-W Series 1-59).

Ambedkar, in his note to the Indian Franchise Committee was emphatic that the application of the literal test of untouchability would be viewed as an attempt to reduce the strength of the depressed classes. He regarded it erroneous to exclude from the category those Untouchables who had taken to cleaner occupations or become comparatively rich. For, he asserted, "Once an untouchable always an untouchable has been the rule of Hindu social life" (Gupta 1985:16-18).

Hindu reformers

In contrast to the British stress on politics and numbers, Hindu reformers beginning with Dayanand Saraswati viewed untouchability as a social problem, internal to Hindu society. The *Indian Review,* a nationalist journal published from Madras, carried a series of articles on the subject between 1909 and 1911 by leading reformers, including Sayajirao Gaikwad of Baroda, G. A. Natesan, T. V. Seshgiri Aiyer and Lala Lajpat Rai. Several English educated caste Hindus set up Depressed Class associations in the provinces. Narayanrao Chandavarkar and Vitthal Ramji Shinde, for instance, founded the Depressed Classes Mission in Bombay Presidency in 1906. The Baroda ruler organized a conference attended, among others, by Bipin Chandra Pal, Vitthalbhai Patel and Lokmanya Tilak, where the demand for the removal of untouchability was made.

Gandhi, who after his return from South Africa in January 1915 dedicated himself to the eradication of the practice, emphasized the moral and religious dimensions of the problem, in comparison to which the political issue "dwindles into insignificance" (Pyarelal 1932: 100). In a letter to the British Prime Minister from Yeravda Jail protesting the Communal Award's grant of separate electorates to the Depressed Classes, he wrote, "Do you realize that if your decision stands and the constitution comes into being, you arrest the marvelous growth of the work of Hindu reformers, who have dedicated themselves to the uplift of their suppressed brethren in every walk of life?" (Gandhi1972 vol. LI: 29-30). Gandhi continued to bring his "genuine moral passion" to the campaign against untouchability to the very end (Mendelsohn and Vicziany 1998: 107). After 1917, however, with the visit of the Secretary of State, Lord Montague, to India in preparation for the next phase of constitutional reforms, the issue of Depressed Class representation in the future political arrangements became predominant.

Joint versus separate electorates

A central issue was whether the Depressed Classes should be granted franchise in a joint electorate with Hindus or through separate electorates a la the Muslims. In an initial articulation of views, Narayanrao Chandavarkar, at a meeting organized by the Depressed Classes Mission in Bombay in November 1917 around the time of the Secretary of State's visit, demanded reservation of seats according to population strength for the Depressed Classes (Zelliot 1988: 183-184). Though unintended, this was a furtherance of the British objective of politicizing the problem of untouchability and according a separate political identity to the Depressed Classes.

The debate however formally commenced in 1919 when the Franchise (Southborough) Committee, entrusted with determining the electoral franchise under the Montague-Chelmsford Reforms, invited members of Depressed Class associations to present their views. B. R. Ambedkar, the sole

Depressed Class graduate in Bombay Presidency, also expressed a desire to testify before the Committee (Khairmode 1955 vol. II: 277). He advised the British to "either … reserve seats…for those minorities that can not, otherwise, secure personal representation or grant communal electorates" (Ambedkar 1989 vol. I: 247-280). In a supplementary written statement, he pressed for a "community electorate" for the Depressed Classes (Ambedkar 1989 vol. I: 270-273). Fellow Mahar, G A Gawai, made a similar presentation (Zelliot 1970: 40). Vitthal Ramji Shinde recommended reserved seats for the Depressed Classes in the general constituencies.

In its ruling, the Southborough Committee proclaimed that, "we intend to make the best arrangement we can for their (the Depressed Classes) representation, in order that they too may ultimately learn the lesson of self-protection" (Mendelsohn and Vicziany 1998: 99). The Government of India Act of 1919 conceded the Depressed Classes one nominated member in the Bombay Legislative Council.

Almost a decade later, as part of an exercise mandatory every ten years, the seven- member Simon Commission was constituted to ascertain Indian opinion on further constitutional advance. While sixteen of the eighteen Depressed Class associations that appeared before the Commission were inclined towards separate electorates (Zelliot 1970: 45), Ambedkar, on behalf of the *Bahishkrit Hitkarni Sabha* he founded in 1924, made an unambiguous plea for universal suffrage and a joint electorate with reservation of seats. He argued,

"Assuming … that separate interests do exist, the question is, are they better promoted by separate electorates than by general electorates and reserved seats? My emphatic answer is that the separate or special interests of any minority are better promoted by the system of general electorates and reserved seats than by separate electorates… this must be said with certainty that a minority gets a larger advantage under joint electorates than it does under a system of separate electorates. With separate electorates the minority gets its own quota of representation and no more. The rest of the house owes no allegiance to it and is therefore not influenced by the desire to meet the wishes of the minority. The minority is thus thrown on its own resources and as no system of representation can convert a minority into a majority, it is bound to be overwhelmed. On the other hand, under a system of joint electorates and reserved seats the minority not only gets its quota of representation but something more. For, every member of the majority who has partly succeeded on the strength of the votes of the minority, if not a member of the minority, will certainly be a member for the minority. This, in my opinion, is a very great advantage which makes the system of mixed electorates superior to that of the separate electorates as a means of protection of the minority " (Ambedkar 1982 vol. II: 351-352).

Ambedkar reiterated these views at the first meeting of the All India Depressed Classes Conference (he founded in opposition to the All India Depressed Classes Association led by M.C. Rajah), in Nagpur on 8 August 1930 in preparation of the first Round Table Conference. Separate electorates, he stated, were not necessary if adult franchise and reservation of seats were granted and legal remedies instituted against untouchability. The Conference passed a resolution approving his stand (*The Bombay Chronicle* 18-8-1930).

Round Table Conference

Meanwhile, the Simon Commission recommended a joint electorate and reservation of seats for the Depressed Classes, the fitness of Depressed Class candidates to be certified by provincial governors. The Congress boycott of the Commission on the ground that it included no Indian member, however, rendered its recommendations redundant. At this juncture, the British convened a Round Table Conference in London. The timing of the Conference raised suspicions that its real purpose was to undermine the nationalist fervour generated by Mahatma Gandhi's mass movements by propping up leaders championing sectional interests. Thereby was the Indian National Congress to be downgraded to one among many parties.

Though, in the absence of the Congress, nothing substantive could be achieved at the Round Table Conference, the game plan was clear. Nationalist leaders would be pitted against nominated leaders not actively engaged in the freedom struggle and with little claim to popular support. Soon after came the announcement of the Gandhi-Irwin Pact, in retrospect a British manoeuvre to secure the Mahatma's commitment to Congress attendance at the second Round Table Conference. The Congress was unenthusiastic about the Pact (Nayar 1995: 331-333) but for inexplicable reasons agreed to Gandhi's participation in London as the sole representative of the party.

B.R. Ambedkar and R. Srinivasan were nominated to represent the Depressed Classes. Srinivasan's selection was intriguing, given that M.C. Rajah, of the same Presidency, had a higher status and was the only Depressed Class member of the Central Legislative Assembly (Keer 1971:195).

According to newspaper reports, several Depressed Class leaders and associations disputed Ambedkar's claims to speak on behalf on the community in London. In Bombay, a section led by the famous cricketer, P. Balu, and B.J. Deorukhkar resolved to cable to the British Premier that the Depressed Classes were with the Congress and opposed to separate electorates. Two largely attended public gatherings in Poona also took a stand against Ambedkar's leadership. Depressed Class members of the United Provinces Legislative Council, in a telegram to London, endorsed adult franchise and a joint electorate. A similar move was reported from Ahmadabad. A huge meeting in Bombay, presided by Sakharam Buwa, recorded its approval of adult franchise and a joint electorate and noted that at Nagpur, Ambedkar had taken a similar stance. The meeting was of the view that whatever the past mistakes of caste Hindus, Gandhi and the Congress had resolved to erase the blot of untouchability. It was, therefore, futile to perpetuate class hatred by demanding separate electorates. The meeting also noted that in London Dr. Ambedkar had found "strange bed-fellows in Maulana Shaukat Ali and other reactionaries" (Source 1982 vol. I: 53- 60).

Minorities Pact

A Minorities Committee was constituted at the Round Table Conference to discuss representation of Muslims and the Depressed Classes in the new constitutional arrangements. Dr. Ambedkar inexplicably abandoned his earlier advocacy of a joint electorate with reservations. He openly aligned with the Muslim, Anglo-Indian and Christian members of the Committee to draft a Minorities Pact, which included among its recommendations separate electorates for the Depressed Classes, with the proviso that the issue be put to a referendum within twenty years. The Pact was a triumph of British stratagems to detach the Depressed Classes from Hindu society. Despite the outcry it generated, Dr. Ambedkar appears not to have offered any reason for abruptly forsaking his previous position.

Mahatma Gandhi, in a strident denunciation of the Minorities Pact, questioned Ambedkar's eligibility to speak for all the Untouchables of India. He declared, "I would not seal the vital interests of the Untouchables even for the sake of winning the freedom of India.... I would fear rather that Hinduism died than that untouchability lived... (The Minorities Pact) will create a division in Hinduism which I cannot possibly look forward to with any satisfaction...I cannot possibly tolerate what is in store for Hinduism if there are two divisions set forth in the villages. Those who speak of the political rights of Untouchables do not know their India, do not know how Indian society is today constructed, and therefore I want to say with all the emphasis that I can command that if I was the only person to resist this thing I would resist it with my life" (Ambedkar 1982 II: 662-663).

Subsequently, in a letter to Sir Samuel Hoare (11-3-1932) Gandhi detailed his position, "I am not against their representation in the legislatures. I should favour everyone of their adults, male or female, being registered as voters irrespective of educational or property qualifications, and that even though the franchise test may be stricter for others" (Pyarelal 1932: 98-103). But separate electorates, he contended, would tear apart Hindu society.

M.C. Rajah pointed out that besides the permanent schism the Minorities Pact would create in Hindu society, it did not concede the Depressed Classes their rightful share of seats as per their numerical strength (*The Hindu* 19-4-1932). The Depressed Classes were granted a small weightage in the Bombay and Madras Presidencies, the home states respectively of Ambedkar and Srinivasan, but in Bengal, Punjab, United Provinces and the Central Provinces the community was given short shrift (for details see Nayar 1996: 33).

In a statement (31-3 1932), G.M. Thaware, Assistant General Secretary of the All India Depressed Classes Association, described the Minorities Pact as beneficial to Muslims and detrimental to the Depressed Classes. In contrast to the Muslims who would get an astounding 177 seats more than their due, the Depressed Classes were asked to settle for 59 seats less, a patently inequitable situation, he stated.

P.N. Rajbhoj (a Chambhar from Maharashtra), in a letter to the private secretary of the Viceroy (7-6-32), asserted that the Depressed Classes in general and the Chambhar and Mang communities in particular, did not recognize Dr Ambedkar and R. Srinivasan as their spokesmen insofar as they advocated separate electorates. Only some months earlier, Rajbhoj pointed out, Ambedkar had taken a stand against separate electorates. The sudden reversal of his position at the Round Table Conference came as a shock to his associates.

Further, Rajbhoj argued, all social movements among the Depressed Classes were based on the premise that they were Hindus and any conflict between them and caste Hindus was an internal affair. Efforts at unification, for which both groups were striving, would receive a setback if separate electorates were implemented. Untouchables would be delivered to the hands of the Muslims whose friendship, he claimed, was more harmful than the indifference of the Hindus.

Rajbhoj added that communities other than the Mahars had never expressed allegiance to Dr. Ambedkar and "are more ill at ease when in the company of his community than in that of the higher classes." Ambedkar, he alleged, did "not even deign to look to the proposals sought to be placed before him by the representatives of smaller Depressed communities…" They feared for their interests under him.

The charge of being a Mahar leader was levelled again at a Chambhar conference in 1939 (*The Bombay Chronicle* 4-7-1939). Two years later, D.N. Kamble, the first educated Mang in the Nizam's state, repeated the accusation. By then the conversion movement among the Mahars had further alienated other Depressed Class groups (Zelliot 1970: 51,67; 1992: 126). The Chambhars of Bombay viewed it as a tactic to enhance the political fortunes of the Mahars (Gokhale 1993: 167).

Ambedkar seeks endorsement of separate electorates

On his return from the Round Table Conference, Ambedkar attempted to create an opinion in favour of separate electorates among the Depressed Classes. He prepared a set of model answers to a questionnaire issued by the Franchise (Lothian) Committee, which he asked sundry Depressed Class associations to forward to the Committee with their signatures (*The Bombay Chronicle* 23-2-1932). On 13 February, he wrote to G.A. Gawai, General-Secretary of the All India Depressed Classes Association, on Rajah's deposition before the Lothian Committee in support of a joint electorate. Therein he asserted that the Lothian Committee was not authorized to discuss the question of electorates with individuals or associations and threatened "breach between us and war amongst ourselves" (*The Bombay Chronicle* 27-2-1932).

Rajah-Moonje Pact

Meanwhile the impasse created by the Minorities Pact prompted the British Prime Minister, Ramsay MacDonald, to ask members of the Minorities Committee to sign a requisition authorizing him to settle the issue. In a letter to the Prime Minister dated 14 November, 1931, Gandhi regretted his inability to accede to the suggestion. Expressing his opposition to any further extension of the principle of separate electorate or special statuary reservation, he said there were other ways of ensuring the election of deserving candidates through the ordinary electorate (Nayar 1996:44).

In February 1932, before the announcement of the Prime Minister's award, came news of an agreement between M.C. Rajah and B.S. Moonje on a joint electorate with reservation of seats on population basis for the Depressed Classes. In his letter to the Prime Minister (*The Hindustan Times*, 25-3-32), Rajah highlighted the historic significance of the accord between "the only central organisation of the Depressed Classes" and "the organised body of Hindus, taken as a whole." He hailed the "hand of fraternity" extended by "our co-religionists, the caste Hindus" as a pointer to their awakening social conscience.

Rajah also set forth the factors that prompted the All India Depressed Classes Association to jettison its earlier demand for separate electorates. That demand, he said, had been made at a time when power still rested with the British who could arbitrate, whenever the need arose, in the interest of the Depressed Classes. But, in the changed context of impending provincial autonomy, separate electorates would place the Depressed Classes "permanently in the opposition." Their representatives could hope for a share in the governance of the provinces only when they merged in a common electorate and subscribed to a common political view. Rajah clarified that even a joint electorate with reservation of seats was "a temporary expedient" till the Depressed Classes, which were an integral constituent of Hindu society, were able to stand on their own.

Writing to the Viceroy (3-6-1932), Thaware, a Mahar leader from Nagpur, pointed out that before finalizing the agreement the consent of the Working Committee of the All India Depressed Classes Association and other Depressed Class leaders had been obtained. Ambedkar, by contrast, appeared to have secured the approval of only R. Srinivasan. Moreover, while the Minorities Pact granted the Depressed Classes 59 seats less than their share and the Provincial Governments in their recommendations to the Indian Franchise Committee proposed still fewer seats, the Rajah-Moonje Pact gave the Depressed Classes 185 seats in the provincial legislatures, 38 in the Upper Chamber and 57 in the Lower Chamber.

Support for Rajah-Moonje Pact

Meanwhile, the Viceroy, in his communication to the Secretary of State (5-3-1932), noted the considerable endorsement Rajah-Moonje Pact had received in the Hindu press. *The Hindustan Times* (29- 2- 1932), while welcoming the resolution of the Working Committee of the All India Depressed Classes Association in favour of a joint electorate, regretted its failure to present a fighting programme. "And it was a fighting programme that the All India Depressed Classes Association should have devised, in consideration of the serious nature of the disruptive forces that have been released by Dr. Ambedkar and his following, however small or insignificant they might be." Dr. Ambedkar, it stated, "has followed his own methods and convictions regardless of the major interests of those he claims to represent...(He) is tenaciously attempting to communalise the depressed classes for all practical purposes, for all time to come, thereby perpetuating the stigma of untouchability on its brow..."

The *Indian Daily Mail* (9-3-1932) held that Dr. Ambedkar "wants to give statutory sanction to the 'Depressed Classes' so that he can raise himself to eminence on their humiliations. To relegate these classes permanently to the backwaters of Hinduism, would not only be a blunder but a gross crime which every Indian, to whatever community he may belong, ought not to countenance for a moment."

The Bombay Chronicle (2-4-1932), commented that Dr. Ambedkar was "audacious enough" to claim that the Depressed Classes had repudiated the Rajah-Moonje Pact and that the All India Depressed Classes Association was a paper organization. This contention, it stated, was so extravagant that it did not merit discussion. The paper noted that 145 associations had endorsed a memorandum in favour of a joint electorate submitted to the Franchise (Lothian) Committee by B.J. Deorukhkar and other leaders. The All India Depressed Classes Association, it further pointed out, had been recognized for the past six-seven years as one of the largest, if not the largest, organization of the Depressed Classes and had a membership of roughly 40,000 (Sources 1982 vol. I: 75-76).

Newspapers reported (*Leader* 23-3-1932) that Lord Lothian, Chairman of the Franchise Committee, and his colleagues were struck by the enthusiasm for the Rajah-Moonje Pact among the Depressed Classes. They were particularly impressed by the pro-Pact procession in Bombay in which demonstrators carried placards bearing slogans like "Long Live Rajah-Moonje Pact," "We Don't Want Separate Electorates," "Down With Dr. Ambedkar" (*Indian Daily Mail* 18-3-1932).

The Lothian Committee also appreciated the significance of the recently concluded elections in Madras Presidency under the Madras District Boards Act, which gave the Depressed Classes a joint electorate with reservation of seats. In Chingleput district, for instance, nominees of the Depressed Classes Association had won the two reserved seats and were hopeful of winning a couple of non-reserved seats as well (*Leader* 23-3-1932).

Why joint electorate?

While Dr. Ambedkar remained silent on the reasons for his transformation into a proponent of separate electorates, Rajah and his colleagues publicly proclaimed their motives for moving in the reverse direction. Separate electorates, Rajah repeatedly emphasized (*The Hindustan Times* 1-5-32), would have protected the interests of the Depressed Classes under the system of dyarchy, but under the proposed provincial autonomy would compel them to "play a second fiddle to one or another party," and hinder their integration in any. It would also deprive them of the opportunity "which will come sooner or later" of sharing in the governance of the provinces.

G.M. Thaware (31-3 1932) reiterated that the Prime Minister's speech at the Round Table Conference announcing provincial autonomy was the catalyst for his Association's shift to a joint electorate after twelve years of demanding separate electorates. Under majority rule in the provinces, the minorities would be unable to overcome the Hindu majority even if they acted in unison. In the Central Provinces, for instance, according to the government's proposal, of the hundred seats,

10 were to be allotted to Muslims

10 to the Depressed Classes and Labour combined

3 to Christians

2 to the hill tribes

making a total of 25. The remaining seventy-five seats would go to caste Hindus who would constitute the permanent majority. The welfare of the Depressed Classes thus demanded that they always be with the Hindus. Untouchability would not disappear, Thaware added, were the Depressed Classes to become a distinct community.

Alluding to Dr. Ambedkar's limited support base, Thaware, pointed out that at the time of founding his All India Depressed Classes Conference in Nagpur in 1930, Ambedkar had pledged to convene a large session that would be attended by over ten lakh delegates. No session was however held in 1931 and the March meet postponed to April. Ambedkar, he alleged, had lacked the confidence to hold a session in Bombay, or any other place except Nagpur, in these two years (on the comparative support base of the All India Depressed Classes Association and the All India Depressed Classes Conference see Thaware's letter to the Viceroy dated 3-6-1932).

The Kamptee Conference

In May 1932, Ambedkar, in a bid to shore up his position, summoned the second session of the All India Depressed Classes Conference at Kamptee, Nagpur, to demonstrate support for the Minorities Pact vis-a-vis the Rajah-Moonje Pact. Members of the All India Depressed Classes Association were not invited though some attended in their individual capacity. In a clash between the two camps at Nagpur station, Thaware and S.M. Mate were injured and other Rajah backers taken into police custody.

Press reports (*Leader*, 11-5-1932) indicate that about 30 delegates from outside Nagpur attended the Conference — 4 from Bengal, 5 from Punjab, 7 from United Provinces, 4 each from Bombay and Madras and 1 from Bihar. Nearly 1,500 Mahars from Nagpur and Kamptee and a sizeable number of labourers from the Empress and Modern mills were also present. A posse of policemen was posted inside and outside the *pandal* to forestall any disturbance.

As the proceedings commenced, P.N. Rajbhoj and Shankar Rao Patil of Poona questioned the legality of the Conference and were manhandled. The vice-president of the reception committee and the city magistrate came to their rescue and escorted them out of the *pandal*. Rajbhoj had to be taken to hospital.

The President of the Conference, Muniswamy Pillay, member of the Legislative Council of Madras, delivered an address in favour of separate electorates wherein he derided Gandhi and the Congress. He turned down repeated requests by proponents of a joint electorate for time to present their views, describing them as hirelings of caste-men. Only the intervention of the police prevented the situation from taking an ugly turn. The press speculated that the refusal to give time probably stemmed from the fear of the organizers that it would divide the gathering. Ambedkar conspicuously maintained silence during the melee. A resolution endorsing the Minorities Pact and repudiating the Rajah-Moonje Pact was passed without being put to vote.

Subsequently in his letter of 3-6-1932, Thaware pointed out that it was police assistance that enabled Ambedkar to hold the conference. No Ambedkar supporter was arrested for violence while the police detained several advocates of a joint electorate.

Communal Award

Soon after the Kamptee Conference, on May 26, Dr. Ambedkar, uneasy due to the enthusiastic endorsement of the Rajah-Moonje Pact by the Depressed Classes, apprehensive of the findings of the Lothian Committee which were perceived as unfavourable to him and unsure of the forthcoming British verdict, secretly left for London to meet the Prime Minister and his colleagues (Source 1982 vol. I: 80-82). He was, however, spotted by a correspondent of *The Bombay Chronicle* while boarding the ship. In London, Ambedkar again pleaded for separate electorates and submitted a twenty-two pages representation to the Cabinet (Keer 1971: 202). Rumours of an impending visit to London by Dr. Moonje and M.C. Rajah added to Ambedkar's anxieties and he directed his followers in Bombay to give Rajah a black send-off if he left from that city (Keer 1971: 203).

Meanwhile, on 17 August 1932 (perhaps in tandem with Ambedkar who returned to India that very day), the British Government announced its Communal Award whereby separate electorates, so far conferred on Muslims, were also granted to the Depressed Classes. To ward off charges that it was consciously attempting to splinter Hindu society, the Award provided a dual vote to the Depressed Classes — one in the general electorate to elect a candidate from the general constituency and another in a separate electorate exclusively of the Depressed Classes to elect a Depressed Class candidate. The number of seats reserved by the Award was not significant, a mere 71 of a total of 1600 in the provincial legislatures. What was pertinent was the calculated bid to detach the Depressed Classes from Hindu society right after an agreement between the two. As the *Bombay Chronicle* (18-8-1932) put it, the Award turned the national majority of the Hindus into a minority.

Mahatma Gandhi received news of the Award in jail on 17 August. In an immediate response he told Mahadev Desai, "...this time they (the British) have created such divisions, conspired to disrupt the country to such a degree, that it may never recover from it" (Nayar 1996: 58)

The following day, Gandhi wrote to the Prime Minister that unless separate electorates for the Depressed Classes were withdrawn he would commence a fast unto death from 20 September, "...as a man of religion that I hold myself to be, I have no other course left open to me..."(Ambedkar 1989 vol. V: 336). Rejecting the argument that the Award had been conferred for twenty years only, Gandhi said, "once the legislatures come into being who can possibly alter the schism caused?"[2]

Gandhi told Lt. Colonel E.E. Doyle, Inspector General of Prisons, Bombay, who visited him in jail on 26 August that, "The Depressed Classes had been given Separate Electorates, when, as a class they did not desire them. A very small minority, the Mahars, under the leadership of Doctor Ambedkar demanded Separate Electorates, but they were not entitled to speak for the Depressed Classes as a whole, who, in the United Provinces, Bengal and elsewhere had definitely declared for Joint Electorates"(N.A.I.: File KW to F 31/113/ 1932 Poll III).

Secret correspondence between the Viceroy and the provincial Governors on the reaction to the Communal Award and the Mahatma's intended fast testified to the correctness of Gandhi's claim. Far from being votaries of separate electorates, the Depressed Classes were mostly unaware of the Award. In a telegram to the Secretary of State on 23 August 1932, the Viceroy acknowledged, "We recognize that at a later stage His Majesty's Government may be forced to make up their minds what in fact the views of the Depressed Classes are, but, in our opinion, they should not take any initiative in the matter..." (N.A.I.: File KW to F 31/113/1932 Poll).

A week later, on 30 August, the Governor of the Central Provinces, A E Nelson, in a confidential letter to the Viceroy noted, "... the bulk of them (the Depressed Classes) are backward and illiterate and are incapable of giving an opinion on the question of joint versus separate electorates...Such depressed class opinion as there is consists of the opinion of about half a dozen leaders, who are followers either of Dr. Ambedkar or Mr. Rajah. They have no settled convictions as they have transferred their allegiance several times from one to the other of these two gentlemen..." (N.A.I.: File KW to F 31/113/1932 Poll IV).

The Governor of Bihar and Orissa, J.D. Sifton, sent a similar assessment sent the following day, "...they (the Depressed Classes) are, in this province, entirely unorganized: except in a few thanas, where experiments are being made in the preparation of electoral rolls on the Lothian plan, the majority are not aware that they are to have any franchise at all, and certainly not that they are offered a separate electorate...The truth is that they are not at present in Bihar and Orissa 'class conscious,' as they are elsewhere in India" (N.A.I.: File KW to F 31/113/1932 Poll IV).

The authorities in Madras, in a communication dated 23 September 1932, made the same point, "...the majority of the Depressed Classes in this Presidency, being mainly uneducated and unorganized, know little or nothing of the trend of political events, understand little or nothing of what they are told and are generally indifferent to what is going on outside their immediate sphere..." (N.A.I.: File 199/32-R). Gandhi's indictment at the Round Table Conference that separate electorates were "a modern manufacture of Government" was clearly not without substance.

Ambedkar, however, defended the Communal Award for its valuable gifts of separate electorates and double vote. Separate electorates, he said, would ensure that only genuine representatives of the Depressed Classes were elected while the dual vote was "a priceless privilege. Its value as a political weapon was beyond reckoning. The voting strength of the Untouchables in each constituency is one to ten. With this voting strength free to be used in the election of caste Hindu candidates, the Untouchables would have been in a position to determine, if not dictate, the issue of the General Election" (Ambedkar 1991 vol. IX: 90).

The argument was not without flaws. As Rajah pointed out (*The Times Of India* 17-7-1932), while the Depressed Classes stood to gain 90 of the 1436 seats in the provincial legislatures according to recommendations of the Indian Central Committee; 177 as per the Simon Commission; and 237 under the Minorities Pact to which Ambedkar himself was a signatory, the Communal Award granted them a mere 71 seats.

Rajah presented a trenchant critique of the Award in the Central Legislative Assembly on 13 September. He stated "...The position we took was that under the scheme of government in which Indians would rule, our safety lay not in finding channels for voicing our opinions, but in taking our due share in the governing of the country. Indeed this is my chief attack on the Premier's letter to Mahatma Gandhi. He tells us that he has given separate electorates for twenty years to enable us to get the minimum number of seats to place our views before the Government and legislature of the day. I contend that this privilege we have already enjoyed under the Montford reforms which have enabled us to get representation in numerous local bodies and in legislatures both provincial and central. We are sufficiently organized for that purpose and do not need either special pleading or special succour. In future what we do need as real remedy for our uplift is definite power to elect our representatives from the general constituencies and hold them responsible to us for their actions. I do not know why the Prime Minister calls the scheme of joint electorates with reservation of seats as impracticable. It is already in force in local bodies in Madras and some other provinces and has worked very satisfactorily. I contend, Sir, that the scheme enunciated in the communal decision involves our segregation and makes us politically untouchables. I am surprised at the argument of the Prime Minister that there is no segregation because we can vote for Caste Hindus who will have to solicit our votes. But, Sir, how can we bring about a common ideal of citizenship when Depressed Class representatives are not to solicit votes of higher castes?"

"...The sufferings which my community has undergone at the hands of Caste Hindus have been acknowledged by Caste Hindus themselves, and I am prepared to admit that there are a large number of reformers among them who are doing everything possible to improve our status and position. I am convinced that there is a change of heart and a in the angle of vision of Caste Hindus. We, Depressed Classes, feel ourselves as true Hindus as any Caste Hindu can be, and we feel that the moral conscience of the Hindus has been roused to the extent that our salvation lies in bringing about a change from within the main body of Hindu society and not segregating ourselves from them. The course adopted by the Government would certainly arrest the progress of this laudable movement..." (Pyarelal 1932: 248-253).

Gandhi's fast unto death

As Gandhi prepared to fast unto death, public meetings of the Depressed Classes were held in Lahore, Karachi, Lucknow and Nagpur in a display of solidarity with the Mahatma (Kumar1987: 96). *The Times of India* reported from Ahmadabad on 15 September, "The news of Mr. Gandhi's resolve to fast unto death has caused a stir among local Depressed Classes over whom Mr. Gandhi has a strong hold by championing their cause for the last fifteen years...Some of the prominent leaders met last night and sent a deputation to Bombay in order to interview Dr. Ambedkar and request him to come to terms with Mr. Gandhi so that he may give up his fast..." In Calcutta, eleven organizations of the Depressed

Classes passed a resolution against the Award, which did not grant adequate representation to the Depressed Classes but brought about their statutory separation from Hindu society. They appealed to Gandhi to withdraw his fast and requested the Government to permit the affected parties to resolve the issue themselves.

In a statement from jail on 16 September, Gandhi said his fast was "intended to sting Hindu conscience into right religious action... No compromise which does not ensure the fullest freedom to the 'depressed classes' inside the Hindu fold can be an adequate substitute for the contemplated separation…" He concluded by stating, "Since there appears to be a misunderstanding as to the application of my fast, I may repeat that it is aimed at a statutory separate electorate, in any shape or form, for the 'depressed' classes. Immediately that threat is removed once for all, my fast will end." Though not enamoured with the idea of statutory reservations, Gandhi expressed his willingness to accept an agreement based on a joint electorate that caste Hindu and Depressed Class leaders might arrive at (Gandhi 1972 LI: 62-65).

As the fast commenced, Madan Mohan Malaviya convened a conference in Bombay on 19 September to hammer out a solution. *The Times of India* reported on the proceedings, "In one instance, it is said, when Dr. Ambedkar claimed the right of negotiating with Mr. Gandhi alone and no one else, Mr. P. Baloo, the Bombay Depressed Class leader from the opposite camp, reminded Dr. Ambedkar that he had no mandate from the community to speak on their behalf." "In another instance," the paper added, "when Dr. Ambedkar declared that if the caste Hindus mobilized their forces, as they sought to do by the holding of that evening's meetings in the city, he would do the same and mobilize every Depressed Class man, woman and child, Mr. Baloo is said to have retorted by saying that Dr. Ambedkar could claim to represent but a single community out of depressed class communities."

Poona Pact

After intense negotiations and frequent consultations with Gandhi, the Poona Pact signed on 24 September 1932 by Madan Mohan Malviya, Tej Bahadur Sapru, M.R.Jayakar, Chunilal Mehta, B.R. Ambedkar, M.C. Rajah, P.G. Solanki, Rajahji, G.D. Birla and twenty others. The Pact did away with separate electorates and gave the Depressed Classes 148 seats as against 78 in the Communal Award. Elections in reserved constituencies were to be held in two phases. In the first, Depressed Class voters would elect a panel of four candidates and, in the second, all voters of the constituency would vote for any one among those short-listed. The first phase was to be operative for ten years, "unless terminated sooner by mutual agreement" and reservations to continue as per the decision of the concerned communities. After the provision of primary elections was abandoned, the Poona Pact became the basis of all subsequent elections (Zelliot 1992: 168).

Given the marked similarity between the Poona Pact and the Rajah-Moonje Pact (Jaffrelot 2005: 67), Ambedkar's rejection of the "less troublesome and more straightforward" Rajah-Moonje Pact remains a puzzle (Keer 1971:216). Critics also wondered why Gandhi at the Round Table Conference did not settle the issue of Depressed Class representation by accepting a joint electorate and reservations (Chimanlal Setalvad *The Times of India* 15-10-1932).

Gandhi clearly spelt out his position in a letter to Rajbhoj written as he commenced his fast. Though reservations were "not open to the same objection" as separate electorates, he said he was absolutely certain that they would "prevent the natural growth of the suppressed classes and will remove the incentive to honourable amends from the suppressers." He elaborated, "What I am aiming at is a heart understanding between the two, the greatest opportunity of repentance and reparation on the part of the suppressers" (Gandhi 1972 LI:

111-112). He wanted nothing less than the removal of the last vestiges of untouchability. If, however, representatives of the suppressed "will not look at my idea" and agreed to statutory reservation of seats, he would not stand in the way. Gandhi's perception that separatism was inherent in reservations appears not too wide off the mark, for the very fact of reservations required the identification and separation of depressed groups. Statutory reservations could thus also be viewed as a victory of British politics. But Gandhi was left without a choice.

British strategists had effectively entrapped him. To have the Communal Award rescinded he had to undergo the ordeal of fast. To rid the country of separate electorates that would create a permanent divide in Hindu society, he had to accept reservations though he was aware of the baneful consequences of reservations on caste lines. Gandhi watched helplessly as his social agenda was upstaged by the political agenda of the British, who successfully thrust untouchability into the arena of power politics. With hindsight it can perhaps be said that had Gandhi and Ambedkar endorsed the Rajah-Moonje Pact, a precursor of the Poona Pact, much of the tension and acrimony that the country witnessed between February and September 1932 could have been avoided.

End-notes

1. Though foiled in 1932, the British continued to entertain the possibility of using the Depressed Classes to weaken the freedom struggle. In a missive to the Viceroy, Lord Linlithgow, dated 16 December 1942, the Secretary of State, Lord Amery, for instance stated, "It does seem to me as if it would be well worth while giving them (the Depressed Classes) a substantial leg-up and assimilating their position increasingly to that of the Muslims. There are, after all, politically very considerable advantages in having two substantial minorities to whom consideration has to be paid, and not to be put in the position of being merely labelled pro-Muslim and anti-Hindu" (Mansergh 1971 III: 390).

The Viceroy, in his letter of 8 February 1943, concurred that "after Gandhi's death, it might be worth considering whether the present anomalous electoral arrangements for the Scheduled Castes should not be altered and a direct communal basis substituted, as originally suggested, but revised up to date in accordance with the census figures..." (Mansergh 1971 III: 633).

The British were, however, troubled by the paucity of leaders among the Scheduled Castes. As Lord Linlithgow observed in a letter to Lord Amery on 5 January 1943, besides Ambedkar, Rajah and Siva Raj, "there are precious few others whom one has heard of in the community" (Mansergh 1971 III: 456).

2. Several years later, in a letter to Rajkumari Amrit Kaur, Gandhi described the Communal Award as "a wicked conspiracy against Indian nationalism." It created, for the first time, "a division amongst Hindus and Hindus while granting separate electorates for the so-called scheduled classes" (Gandhi 1983 LXXXVII: 315).

Select References

National Archives of India, Government of India.

Government of India, Reforms Office

File F111/32-R

Home Political Files

File 31/113/32-Poll and unprinted K-W Series 1-59

File KW to F 31/113/1932 Poll

File KW to F 31/113/1932 Poll III

File KW to F 31/113/1932 Poll IV

File 199/32-R

Ambedkar, B.R. 1946. *Pakistan Or The Partition Of India*, Thacker and Co., Ltd.

-1989. *Writings and Speeches*, vol. I, Government of Maharashtra.

-1982. *Writings and Speeches*, vol. II, Government of Maharashtra.

-1989. *Writings and Speeches*, vol. V, Government of Maharashtra.

-1991. *Writings and Speeches*, vol. IX, Government of Maharashtra.

-1982. *Source Material on Dr. Babasaheb Ambedkar and the Movement of Untouchables*, vol. I, compiled by B. G. Kunte, Government of Maharashtra.

Gandhi, M.K. 1972. *The Collected Works Of Mahatma Gandhi*, vol. LI, The Publications Division, Government of India.

-1983. *The Collected Works Of Mahatma Gandhi*, vol. LXXXVII, The Publications Division, Government of India.

Gokhale, Jayashree. 1993. *From Concessions to Confrontation: The Politics of an Indian Untouchable Community,* Popular Prakashan.

Gopal, Ram. 1964. *Indian Muslims. A Political History (1858-1947),* Asia Publishing House.

Gupta, S.K. 1985. *The Scheduled Castes in Modern Indian Politics: Their emergence as a Political Power*, Munshiram Manoharlal.

Hardy, Peter. 1972. *The Muslims Of British India*, Cambridge University Press.

Jaffrelot, Christophe. 2005. *Dr. Ambedkar and Untouchability,* permanent black.

Keer, D.1971. *Dr. Ambedkar, Life and Mission*, Popular Prakashan.

-1973. *Mahatma Gandhi. Political Saint and Unarmed Prophet,* Popular Prakashan.

Khairmode, D.B. 1955. *Dr. Bhimrao Ramji Ambedkar*, vol. I and II, Pratap Prakashan.

Kumar, Ravinder. 1987. "Gandhi, Ambedkar and the Poona Pact, 1932," in J. Masselos ed., *Struggling and Ruling: The Indian National Congress, 1885-1985,* Sterling Publishers.

Mansergh, Nicholas. ed. 1971. *The Transfer Of Power 1942-47*, vol. III, Her Majesty's Stationery Office.

Mendelsohn, Oliver and Marika Vicziany. 1998. *The Untouchables. Subordination, Poverty And The State In Modern India*, Cambridge University Press.

Nayar, Sushila. 1995. *Mahatma Gandhi*, vol VI, Navajivan Publishing House.

-1996. *Mahatma Gandhi*, vol VII, Navajivan Publishing House.

Omvedt, Gail. 1994. *Dalits and the Democratic Revolution*, Sage.

Pyarelal. 1932. *The Epic Fast*, Navjivan Press.

Rai, Lajpat. 1928. *Unhappy India*, Banna Publishing Company.

Rajah, M.C. 1925. *The Oppressed Hindus,* Huxley Press.

Shourie, Arun. 1998. *Worshipping False Gods*, Harper Collins.

Zelliot, Eleanor. 1970. "Learning the Use of Political Means: The Mahars of Maharashtra," in Rajni Kothari ed., *Caste In Indian Politics*, Orient Longman.

-1988. " Congress and the Untouchables — 1917-1950," in R. Sisson and S. Wolpert eds., *Congress and Indian Nationalism — The Pre-Independence Phase*, Oxford University Press.

-1992. *From Untouchable To Dalit. Essays on Ambedkar Movement*, Manohar.

Section I

Rajah-Moonje Pact
The British Concern*

1. Telegram R. No. 676. dated 1st (recd. 2nd) March 1932.

From ....Secretary of State for India, London.

To.............Viceroy (Reforms Office), New Delhi.

Reforms

Dated 2.3.32

File No.

Serial No. D- 910/R

Reuter reports pact between the Hindu Mahasabha and the Depressed Classes Association regarding representation of the depressed classes in the Legislatures. I should be glad to receive details with any estimates you can give of the extent to which pact is likely to receive general acceptance by interests involved.

(Secy, P.S.V., O., & Dept.)

I have informally consulted the Home Department and the Assistant Director, Intelligence Bureau.

A draft telegram is submitted for approval. Home Department and D.I.B. may see before issue.

LCM

2/3

J.S. The language of the telegram stated to have been sent to the Prime Minister is repeated in the draft. Because the telegram is understood to have been sent to the Prime Minister by name, and may not have been seen in the India Office, who merely cite a Reuter's message.

We shall be grateful for any comments Home Dept. (and the D.I.B.) may wish to make on the draft. The only expression of opinion I have myself yet heard on the pact was from Mr. Srinivasan, the representative of the depressed classes on the Consultative Committee; and he very severely criticised Mr. Rajah (to whom he attributed personal motives which we need not mention to the S. of S.

W.H. Lewis

H.D. 2.3.32

Submitted. There is no information in the office about the Hindu Mahasabha Depressed Classes pact. The file may perhaps be seen by the D.I.B. before any comments on the draft are recorded.

We should be glad of DIB's comments

C.N. Gwynne

3.3.32

I think the draft accurately describes the position. We have practically no further information. Ambedkar "rules" in the South up to Berar, C.P. and part of Bombay. Such influence (small) as Rajah has is confined to the Punjab and Delhi. We would possibly have written "any more than slight" instead of "general" in the penultimate line of the draft.

H. Williamson

4.3.32

C.N. Gwynne

4.3.32

The draft is for approval.

W.H. Lewis

5.3.32

**

2. Telegram R. No. 714, dated 5th March 1932.

From... Viceroy (Reforms Office), New Delhi

To......... Secretary of State for India, London.

Your telegram 676 of 1st March. Hindu Maha Sabha Depressed Classes Pact. We have no information regarding pact or connected details except what has appeared in press reports here, according to which following message is stated to have been sent to Prime Minister by name: Begins. Regarding the demand of separate electorates by Dr. Ambedkar, the Working Committee of the All-India Depressed Classes Association was held in Delhi on 21st and 22nd instant, and unanimously decided for joint electorates with Hindus, with reservation of seats on population basis. Complete agreement now prevails between the Depressed Classes Association and the Hindu Mahasabha. Letter follows. Ends. We are watching progress and will telegraph later any definite information that may become available. We do not at present attach great significance to the pact which is understood to have been brought about by Rajah and Moonje behind closed doors. To judge from evidence so far given before Franchise Committee there is little reason yet to think that Rajah's views will find general acceptance among Depressed Classes. The Hindu press of course is making the most of Rajah's declaration and endeavouring to win the Depressed Classes over to his side.

(P.S.V., O., & Dept.)

Draft (?) forwarding a copy of the telegram from and to the S/S to HD (Home Department) put up for approval.

LCM

Please see the extract from the Hindustan Times at Slip J. For orders whether any further communication should be sent to S/S in continuation of our telegram of the 5th March.

LCM

5/3

We had better await further developments. Resubmit on 12.3

W.H. Lewis

8.3.32

Will office please put on the file relevant extracts from our collections of press cuttings. Tendentious leaders and articles are not of much value. What we want to get at is the extent to which the pact has or is receiving endorsement from various organizations, whether Hindu or Depressed class. Also, have not statements appeared to the effect that the pact has received Sikh support.

W. H. Lewis

14.3.32

Nothing further has appeared in the Press beyond the meeting of the 6th March that took place at Dr. Moonje's residence and in which certain Hindu and Sikh M.L.A.'s took part.

So far we are aware the pact has not yet been endorsed by any organisation of Hindu, Sikh or Depressed Classes.

LCM

15.3

We may defer our further communication to the S.of S till after the arrival in Delhi of the Franchise Committee. The Secretariat of the Committee will probably be able to give us information of the extent to which the Pact is influencing views expressed to the Committee regarding the future representation of the depressed classes.

W. H. Lewis

19.3.32

I have mentioned this to Mr. Laithwaite. We may continue to hold up our further communication to the S.of S till after the 30th inst. when the All India Depressed Classes Association of which Mr. Rajah is President will give evidence before the Franchise Committee

W. H. Lewis

23.3.32

The evidence given by Rajah on behalf of the All-India Depressed Classes Association is put up.

LCM

31.3

I think that we might now wire to Secretary of State somewhat as follows:-

"Reference our telegram of 5th March, No. 714. Rajah Moonje Pact.

Rajah appeared on 30th March as witness before Franchise Committee in support of Pact. General impression is that his claim to speak for majority of community was somewhat shaken in course of his examination by Ambedkar. Organisation of demonstrations both here and in Bombay by Rajah's supporters coupled with propaganda in Nationalist press continues to keep the Pact in foreground, but tendency is to regard issue as primarily of interest for South India only, and at this stage is still confused with personal rivalries of individual leaders."

We shall be grateful for any suggestions Home Department and Director, Intelligence Bureau, may wish to make.

W. H. Lewis

31.3.32

We have nothing further to add.

A meeting of the all India Depressed Classes leaders of pro-pact views may be held shortly at Nagpur. This meeting was not held earlier because of the Franchise Committee meeting at Delhi.

Sd. illegible

1.4.32

It was stated in the telegram of the 5th March that we were watching progress and will telegram later any definite information that might become available. The information contained in the draft suggestion by Mr. Lewis in perhaps not quite definite, and as stated above there is going to be a meeting of the leaders shortly. In these circumstances the communication proposed to be sent to the Secretary of State might perhaps be held up for a short time more.

Sd. illegible

2.4.32

I would suggest that the telegram might he sent with a brief addition as at **'A'** in DIB's note above a with a promise of further communication if this meeting is held, and the position undergoes change.

C.N. Gwynne

2.4.32

Will office please place a draft on the file in terms of my note of the 31st March plus the addition suggested by H.D.

WH Lewis
2.4.32

A draft is placed on the file.

LCM

The draft is for approval.

WH Lewis
4.4.32

**

Telegram R. No. 902., dated 4th April 1932.

3. From........Viceroy (Reforms Office), New Delhi.

To............Secretary of State for India, London.

Reference our telegram of 5th March No. 714. Rajah Moonje Pact. Rajah appeared on 30th March as witness before Franchise Committee in support of Pact. General impression is that his claim to speak for majority of community was somewhat shaken in course of his examination by Ambedkar. Organisation of demonstrations both here and in Bombay by Rajah's supporters coupled with propaganda in Nationalist press continues to keep the pact in foreground, but tendency is to regard issue as primarily of interest for South India only, and at this stage is still confused with personal rivalries of individual leaders.

A meeting of the All India Depressed Classes' leaders of pro-pact views may be held shortly at Nagpur. A further communication will be sent you if this meeting is held and the position undergoes change.

(P.S.V., O., & Dept.)

So far we are aware no meeting of the all India Depressed classes has taken place at Nagpur yet. Newspapers extracts at slip T are of interest.

Mentioned to J.S. Please keep.

LCM

6/5

The all India Depressed Classes Conference was held at Kamptee (Nagpur) on the 7th and 8th May 1932 in a disorderly state. Resolutions were adopted by Dr. Ambedkar's party supporting "Minorities Pact" and repudiating "Rajah-Moonje Pact"- Mr. Rajah's followers did not cooperate with the conference - For orders whether we should address the S/S with references to the last para of our telegram dt. 4/4/32 on p 4 of correspondence.

LCM 12/5

The claim of the All-India Depressed Classes Conference to represent the community is disputed by the All-India Depressed Classes Association (vide article in the "Leader" of the 12th May).

It is clear that opinion among the depressed classes is still divided. My own impression is that neither side has yet succeeded in establishing its claim to speak the mind of the majority.

2. Have Home Dept and D.I.B. any comments to make to the drafts?

W.H. Lewis

13.5.32

We should be glad of the DIB's comments as soon as possible-

C.N. Gwynne

13-5-32

D.I.B.

Although the meeting at Kamptee has shown that Dr. Ambedkar has at present a somewhat larger following than his rival, the Conference in question cannot be called representative of the Depressed Classes, inasmuch as M.C. Rajah's side was not represented, nor was it given an opportunity to argue its case. What rowdyism there was has been much exaggerated in the nationalist press and it would be incorrect to say that the meeting was held "in a disorderly state". One important point about the meeting was that Kalicharan Nandagawli, who has considerable influence in the Nagpur-Bhandara area (an important area where Depressed Classes are concerned) announced his conversion to Ambedkar's policy. The draft cable meets the case.

H. Williamson

16.5.32

**

4. Telegram R. No. 1199., dated 19th May 1932.

From........Viceroy (Reforms Department), Simla.

To............Secretary of State for India, London.

Reference last sentence of our telegram of 4th April 1932. All-India Depressed Classes Conference was held at Nagpur on 7th and 8th instant, when resolutions were passed supporting Ambedkar and Minorities Pact and repudiating Rajah-Moonje Pact. Conference was not attended by Rajah or his party, but some disorder was caused by interruptions of the proceedings by those who support this views. The claim of the Conference to represent the depressed classes is disputed by a rival body designated All-India Depressed Classes Association which has in turn announced its intention to hold an early meeting. It is clear that opinion in the community is still sharply divided and so far as can be seen neither side has yet succeeded in establishing its claim to speak the mind of the majority.

(P.S.V., O., & Dept.)

For information

Are the Poona men influential? The Nagpur man is a henchman of M.C. Rajah.

M. Yeatts

18.6.32

Mr. Thaware is Mr. Rajah's supporter. They are not without influence but no action seems called for.

LCM — M. Yeatts

20/6 — 20.6.32

The anti-Ambedkar body of Depressed Classes held a meeting at Bombay on Sunday, the 10th July, under the presidentship of Rao Bahadur M.C. Rajah. The proceedings are reported in the extract below from the Eastern Times of the 12th July 1932. No further communication need be sent to the Secy. of State, with ref. to our telegram of the 19th May last.

LCM — M. Yeatts

14/7 — 14.7.32

**

*Source N. A. I.: File 111/32-R

Section II

Correspondence and statements of Depressed Class leaders*

5. Statement by G.M. Thaware, Assistant General Secretary, All India Depressed Classes Association, on 31 March 1932.

Salvation of the Depressed Classes Lies in Joint Electorates

Dr. Ambedkar and his followers seem to be very much displeased with the All India Depressed Classes Association as the Association is in favour of the joint electorates and no sooner did Dr. Ambedkar get news that I was in favour of the joint electorates and was to appear on 15-3-1932 as a witness before the Indian Franchise Committee than he sent telegrams to 5 or 6 persons of Central Provinces and Berar requesting them to see him at Bombay. They accordingly assembled at Bombay. They gave me to understand that they were also to be examined as witnesses by the Franchise Committee. Instead of calling any of them, the Committee sent for Mrs. Ramabai Tambe as the next witness after me. Naturally Dr. Ambedkar's party lost all heart and the persons concerned made themselves butt of ridicule.

The All India Depressed Classes Association was started at Nagpur in the year 1926 at the All India Depressed Classes Leaders' Conference when Dr. Ambedkar was invited to attend it. He declined the invitation and Rao Bahadur M.C. Rajah, Member of the Legislative Assembly was approached and was elected president thereof. Rao Bahadur Rajah was elected as President while Dr. Ambedkar and other representatives from each Province elected as Vice-Presidents of the Association. Thereafter, in 1928, it was proposed that Dr. Ambedkar should be elected President of the annual session of the All India Depressed Classes Conference to be held at Delhi. He was invited accordingly. He agreed at first, but only two days prior to the date of the Conference, he sent a telegram requesting the Conveners to postpone the Conference. It was however not postponed and R.B. Rajah was requested to be the president thereof a second time. Dr. Ambedkar's friend Dr. Solanki attended the Conference and himself moved a proposal that there should be two presidents of the All India Depressed Classes Association i.e., R.B. Rajah and Dr. Ambedkar. This proposal failed for want of a seconder and Rao Bahadur Rajah was again elected unanimously as president of the Association. Some time after this, Dr. Ambedkar wrote to me a letter akin to his resignation. I had placed it before the Working Committee. Dr. Ambedkar tried his utmost, to establish, with the aid and co-operation of Mr. Nandagaoli, a separate Association. He soon fell out with Mr. Nandagaoli. At Nagpur in 1930, Dr. Ambedkar himself founded a separate association the so called "All India Depressed Classes Congress" as a rival Association to the "All India Depressed Classes Association". Will it ever be an act of wisdom on the part of the learned gentleman from amongst the Depressed Classes themselves to establish a separate and rival Association when his duty lay in espousing the cause of and foster up the mother and well-organised institution, the All India Depressed Classes Association already established for the benefit of the Depressed Classes all over India?

In 1926 when our Association was founded, we took Dr. Ambedkar along with us as Vice-President. Not only this but we went even further; and we did not fail to invite him to each and every Conference and yet it is not known to this day as to what was the propriety of Dr. Ambedkar's starting this rival body in 1930, for the Depressed Classes. I leave it to others to decide as to who tried to break up our community and who is responsible for the present-day division amongst the Depressed Classes.

By his speech in the session of the Nagpur Congress (1930), Dr. Ambedkar made it known that he was in favour of the joint electorates for the Depressed Classes and a resolution supporting the demand of Joint Electorate was also accordingly passed in that Congress. It is to be remembered that Congress was not at all convened under the auspices of our Association. Dr. Ambedkar himself was the president and it was a creation of his own. When the Simon Commission visited India and while Dr. Ambedkar was a member of its Bombay Co-operation Committee, he was in favour of the joint electorate and actually demanded it when examined as a witness by that Commission. Not only this but he stuck up to his guns even in the first session of the Round Table Conference. But he has not yet disclosed as to what made him change his opinion and become an exponent of the separate electorates at the second Round Table Conference!

I was then in favour of Separate Electorates and my Association was also in favour of the same. Dr. Ambedkar was also for them and thus there was unanimity of opinion amongst us all. Some of the followers of Dr. Ambedkar at Nagpur saw no difficulties in bringing about a compromise between our Association and Dr. Ambedkar. In no less than 5 or 6 public meetings, I myself suggested the ways and means of effecting this compromise. I then proposed to them that the All India Depressed Classes Association was established prior to the Congress founded by Dr. Ambedkar and as there had already been as many as seven annual and two special sessions of the All India Depressed Classes Conference in several parts of India and as the tenth session of it was then about to be held at Gudhgaon in Punjab, under the auspices of my Association they should send a telegram to Gudhgaon and invite the next session at Nagpur. I told them to enlist ten or fifteen thousand members of their opinion and who would help Dr. Ambedkar's election as President of the Association. This was the best way of the compromise but they did not see their way to accept such an excellent proposal of mine. Instead of this his Congress has resolved to hold the session of the

Congress at Kamptee. Dr. Ambedkar said in his presidential speech at his Congress of Nagpur held in 1930 that he would arrange such a large conference so that about ten lakhs of delegates would attend it at his invitation. But we saw in 1931 that there was held no Congress under the auspices of his body and now they are arranging at Kamptee its next session after two years. This Congress was reported to be held in March 1932 but it is postponed without giving any reason to April 1932. Dr. Ambedkar was however conscious about his position and dared not call the next session of his Congress in Bombay or at any other place except Nagpur within these two years. Dr. Ambedkar blue his trumpet from the Presidential chair of the so called All India Depressed Classes Congress at Nagpur and is still busy with doing the same thing that the All India Depressed Classes Association is not a representative body but a paper Association. Grapes were sour to him! He started the All India Depressed Classes Congress in 1930 as a rival Association but does not seem satisfied with it now and is going to start another more representative Association for the Depressed Classes in next session of his Congress in 1932! It seems he admits that his own Congress is a paper Association.

The reasons why we "demand joint electorate"

I have received a number of letters on this subject and many notable persons have already expressed their approval of the system of joint electorate. Ever since the year 1919 right up to the end of the year 1931 we ourselves were in favour of "Separate electorates". For full 12 years we made strenuous efforts in that direction, taking our proportion to the whole population, as the basis into our consideration. But finding that our efforts were all in vain and foreseeing definite ruin in future in clinging fast to it, we have been obliged to change our views. During all these past 12 years we have been telling at the top of our voice that we do not want control over the Army or even the power of the purse but what was wanted was only a few seats in legislatures in proportion to our population. And what has been our experience? The Central Provinces Government recommended only 10 seats for the Depressed Classes and the Labour combined, when according to our proportion to the population of the province we were entitled to get 22 seats. The percentage of the Mohammedans is only 4 and yet they can get 10 seats. Though our percentage is 20, only 10 seats have been recommended for us Depressed Classes covering with labour seats. Is that justice and fair play? Yet curiously enough R.B. Shriniwasan, in consultation with Dr. Ambedkar proposed in his speech at the Second Round Table Conference a reduction of the seats for the Depressed Classes in other provincial Councils and a consequent increase of seats in the Madras and Bombay Councils. When they are not entitled to it according to our proportion to the population there, why should our Province be deprived of our seats and Bombay and Madras be given more seats than their proportion?

We have been charged with having changed our views so soon as that. That however is not so. It took us 12 full years to give up those old views and there are reasons and reasons for that in addition to those that have been already stated above in extenso. The chief reason for such a change is that the Prime Minister in his speech at the Round Table Conference has already spoken of the grant of Provincial Autonomy. There is a world of difference between the system as it obtains today and the proposed Provincial Autonomy. Under the present system the whole administration still rests in the hands of Englishman, the Government can safely give a go by to all that the Council may have decided upon. When we were tyrannized by the Hindus in some villages, we sought the protection of the Government and the same was extended. There are instances of ourselves being tyrannized by other sections of the Hindu community in villages and Government help us when we seek their protection. For this I thank our Government sincerely. But this system of Government is not to obtain over the proposed Provincial Autonomy under which the reigns of Government are to be in the hands of the majority party as we find it at present in the British Parliament. The Hindus are in overwhelming majority in the Provinces and even if the minority communities (the Mahomedans, Christian, and the Depressed Classes and the rest) combine according to the pact of Dr. Ambedkar, they will not be able to overcome the Hindu Majority. For instance, as per Governments's proposal, it is so plain that there will be only 10 seats for Mahomedans, 10 others for the Depressed Classes and Labour, 3 of the Christians and 2 others of the Hill tribes — in all 25 seats are available out of the total number of 100 seats in C.P. The rest of the seats i.e., 75 will be of the Hindus and hence none but they will always command majority. The depressed classes if they separate from the Hindus, will not be able to do anything in the Council. If we are really desirous of doing something worth the name for our community, we shall have always to be with the Hindus. Our aim is to remove untouchability. If we become a distinct community from the Hindus in the next constitution, untouchability will not vanish away at all and there will always be keen animosity and heart burning amongst the untouchables and the other Hindus. The Depressed Classes will gain nothing at all. Under the proposed form of Government, the present diarchy is not to exist at all and in case we separate as a body from the Hindus, it will be very difficult with us to get redressed.

Now, it has been said that under the joint electorate system, only the favourite of the Hindus will always be returned. But the same could as well be said of the system of separate electorate. Suppose for instance that a graduate of the Depressed Classes is a candidate for the District of Bhandara and that the other rival candidate is not a graduate but is an illiterate and wealthy man. It is just likely that the latter due to the purse at his command may be returned. In that case we will be deprived of a graduate candidate who would have been really serviceable; and worthless representative will do nothing beyond merely occupying one seat in the Council by separate electorate. I concede that from a constituency in which there is no movement of ours and the social movement of the Hindus and wherein there is no our capable candidate available, from such backward district a favourite of the Hindus may get into the Council under the joint electorate system. But when there are reformers amongst the Hindus and also capable men amongst us, the deserving one will alone be elected. Rao Bahadur Rajah has already given out his experience in the Madras Presidency, in his letter appearing in the Times of India dated 25th March 1932. The Non-Brahmin party of Madras, demanded separate electorate in 1919 when the Montague-Chelmsford-Scheme was on the anvil. They did not get it, instead they were given the joint electorate with some reserved seats. The result is that the non-Brahmins lost nothing at all. On the contrary we find that as many as 45 candidates of (Non-Brahmin) Justice Party can be elected unopposed and the ministers are also chosen from that party. The same is the case with Central Provinces. The leaders of the Non-Brahmins demanded separate electorate when they were examined by the Simon Commission. But today we find that under the joint electorate system, the Democratic party which is in all a party of the Non-Brahmins so powerful in the Central Provinces Council that combine all other groups may, they could not defeat the Democratic party. The ministers are also from this party. The one who was then demanding separate electorate is himself the leader of the Democratic party today. The Peoples' and the National party both combined, could not defeat the Democratic party. May I ask why should the Depressed Classes not think likewise to happen under the new reforms? We have not seen the appointment of a Mahomedan Minister in our Province as the Mahomedans enjoy separate electorate. One time one Mahomedan Minister was appointed but he was removed in no time. Now we see Mahomedan

President of the Central Provinces Legislative Council elected by the members of the Central Provinces Council. He was elected with the help of Democratic Party i.e., with the help of Hindus and not by seven members of his caste. Some will say that the Depressed Classes will also enjoy the same in separate electorate just as the Mahomedans are enjoying at present. But it is possible in the present diarchy system of the Government and not in the proposed provincial autonomy.

According to the Lucknow Pact between the Indian National Congress and the Mohamedans, the Mohamedans get more seats than they are entitled to according to their proportion to the population, where they could secure these in this manner, why should we the depressed classes not enter into any agreement on similar lines with the Hindu Mahasabha?

It is for this very reason that our Association has changed its view. Our Association is fully convinced that the Separate electorate system is not profitable and hence not suitable. It is suicidal and highly prejudicial to our interests. The joint electorate is beneficial and therein alone our political salvation can be made. The Mohamedans entered into a Pact with the Indian National Congress at Lucknow, Dr. Ambedkar effected a Pact in England, with the minority communities and R.B. Rajah entered into an agreement with Dr. Moonje at new Delhi. Out of these three pacts, New Delhi pact alone is perfect and judicious.

Defects in Dr. Ambedkar's Minority Pact of London

This Pact is not beneficial to the Depressed Classes Communities at all, but it is beneficial to the Mahomedans. Because the Depressed Classes can get according to Dr. Ambedkar's Pact, 59 seats less than their proportion and the Mahomedans get 177 seats more than their proportion. Dr. Ambedkar's Province (Bombay) will get 16 seats more to the Depressed Classes than their proportion and Rao Bahadur

Shrinivasan's Province (Madras) will get 10 seats more to the Depressed Classes than their proportion. But for other Provinces the Depressed Classes will get less seats in their legislatures than their proportion. This is selfishness on the part of Dr. Ambedkar to enter into such sort of unjudicious and imperfect Pact.

It has been suggested that owing to his being very clever Dr. Ambedkar understands things better than others. It may be true in educational qualifications only and not in politics. We come across instances of a quack curing a patient of his disease in no time, which even a very clever physician had not been able to cure him of. The patient, desirous as he is to any way get rid of his disease, prefers the quack's dose to that of a clever and England returned physician. The same is the principle here. Moonje-Rajah Pact seems to be the sovereign balm on the ailment of the depressed classes. It is feared that Dr. Ambedkar's method may aggravate the agamic instead of abating than experience counts more than cleverness.

Rao Bahadur Rajah is one of our educated, capable and experienced leader who has spent more than a decade in politics. He was in the Simon Commission for more than 6 months; and has also spent an equal number of months in politics in England. He is a Statesman with vast experience and I trust he is the real leader of the Depressed Classes. He alone could see wherein lies our salvation.

G.M. Thaware,

Nagpur — Assistant General Secretary

31st March 1932 — All India Depressed Classes Association

**

No.125 of 19326.766

6. The All India Depressed Classes Association

Head Office-Nagpur

Dated 3rd June 1932

To

The Private Secretary,
to his Excellency the Viceroy
Camp India

Sir,

I beg to enclose herewith two copies of the Statements on Joint Electorates for the Depressed Classes for His Excellency's kind perusal and information.

I hope, you will kindly place them before His Excellency, and oblige.

I beg to remain,

Sir,
Your most obedient servant
G.M.Thaware
(Sadar Bazar Nagpur)

Separate Electorates is suicidal

The demand for separate Electorates was made before the Simon Commission by the Depressed Classes, Muslims and Non-brahmins. The Depressed Classes from all other Provinces except Bombay then made a demand for separate Electorates and Dr. Ambedkar alone was in favour of Joint Electorates. But the Simon Commission has in their Report recommended for the Depressed Classes Joint Electorates with reservation of seats and had expressed their opinion that it would remove the untouchability by mixing with the Hindus. Now there are two different parties of the Depressed Classes which advocate joint or separate electorates. But it is ultimately in the hands of the Government either to sanction joint or separate electorates. It will be suicidal for the Depressed

Classes to have separate electorates. For instance today we have 73 Members in the C.P. Legislative Council of which one seat has been kept vacant. Out of 72, ten are Government Officials; eight are nominated (four Depressed Classes; one Labour; one Woman seat; one [? cannot be read] and one Christian); seven Members elected from Mahomedan Constituencies by separate electorates and two others according to the Minority Pact — all there including number twenty-seven. Rest 45 Members are elected from joint non Mahomedan Constituencies and are Hindus. Even with these 27 Members out of 72, no Muslim or a Parsi can be appointed as a Minister; but during the last ten years there have been Ministers only from the Hindus. Now I challenge Dr. Ambedkar to explain how it is possible to appoint a Muslim, Christian or a Depressed Classes Minister when in the new Council of the C.P., there will be 100 Members out of which only 23 Members will be of the Minority Communities such as Depressed Classes, Christians and Muslims and 77 seventy-seven Hindu Members. In the Report of the Sub-Committee of the Second Round Table Conference, on page 61 Column 7; Dr. Ambedkar has agreed in his Minority Pact to have appointed a Minister from Muslims or any other Minorities of considerable number by convention. But the C.P. Council in the next Reforms will have only 23 seats for the Minorities. Now is it possible then to appoint such Ministers or to decide that 23 is a considerable number?

There are examples of 4 or 5 Municipalities like Nagpur, Hinganghat and others in C.P. that Muslims have been elected as Presidents in the present system of the General Electorates of the Local Bodies. Therefore what is the need of Separate Electorates even for the Muslims? With the increase of the Franchise of the voters of the Local Bodies, it has made possible to appoint a Depressed Classes (Mahar) Secretary or Vice President for the Civil Station Sub-Committee of the Nagpur Municipality. Similarly there are examples of Umrer

(Nagpur) and Akola Local Boards where two capable Members from the Depressed Classes have been elected by the majority of Hindu votes. These two Members are not the underlings of the Hindus. Therefore it is not profitable to have Separate Electorates of the Depressed Classes.

Loyalists and Extremists

It is useless to say that those who advocate Separate Electorates are Loyalists and those who advocate Joint Electorates are extremists. The whole Depressed Classes Community is loyal to the British Government and therefore the Government should entertain no fear on that account. It is not clear whether the C.P. Government has recommended Separate or Joint Electorates for the Depressed Classes. The Bombay Government has recommended for the Depressed Classes Separate Electorates and the present attitude of the Government seems to be in favour of Separate Electorates for these Classes. It is due to the Police aid that Dr. Ambedkar's Kamptee Depressed Classes Congress could be successful. At the first Meeting, convened by the advocates of joint electorates in the Town Hall Nagpur, the supporters of separate electorates showed black flags and even threw a shoe in the meeting but no follower of separate electorates was taken into custody by the Police. When the supporters of Joint electorates showed black Flags to the supporters of separate electorates at Nagpur Station, 5 persons were taken into custody by the same police and in Kamptee on the first day of the Congress, 2 persons were seriously beaten by the Congress-men in the Pandal but the Police did not intervene even after beating the supporters of joint electorates. I understand that a notice has been served to one of the advocates of joint electorates at Poona by the Dist Magistrate so that he should not interfere in the work of Dr. Ambedkar. Such sort of attitude of the Police is condemnable.

The Duty of the Government

It was the duty of the Government to give to the Minority Communities full weightage if the Minorities were to be really benefited by the Government. We had no objection in giving seats to the Muslims, Indian Christians, Anglo-Indians and Europeans three times more than their proportion of population, but the Depressed Classes ought to have been given at least proportionate representation on their population basis if not more in all Legislatures, by the Government. That is the reason behind the fact that the Government Official Members of the Provincial Franchise Committees objected to recommend proportionate representation on the population basis for the Depressed Classes? According to the population of these Classes they should get 304 seats. The Minority Pact of London has recommended 59 seats less than their proportion i.e. 245 only and the Provincial Franchise Committees in their recommendations to the Indian Franchise Committee have suggested nearly half seats less than the number suggested in the Minority Pact. This is what we have obtained our loyalty. In order to please the Hindu Extremists, is it the justice of the Government to offer them the Posts of three to four thousand rupees per month? If the Government were in fact desirous in benefiting the Minority Communities, they ought to have recommended as below so that there would be the majority of the representatives of the minority Communities in all the Legislatures in the next Reforms. Majority of the minority Communities cannot be formed in the Legislatures such as Upper Chamber, Bihar and Orissa, C.P., Madras etc. by the Pact of the Minorities made at London.

Strength of cham	Caste	Depress. Classes	Total	Mus. lim	Chris. tians	Sikh	Anglo Indians	Trib als etc.	Euro peans	Majority of the representations of the Minority communties
Centre										
All India										
(1931)	(47.5)	(19)*	(66.5)	(21.5)						
Upper200	88	50	138	50	1	6	1	-	4	112 against 88
Lower300	128	70	198	70	7	10	3	-	12	172 against 128
	(48.9)	(13.4)	(62.3)	(34.8)						
Assam100	38	13	51	35	3	-	1	-	10	62 against 38
	(18.3)	(24.7)	(43)	(44.8)						
Bengal200	36	45	81	94	2	-	3	-	20	164 against 36
Bihar&	(67.8)	(14.5)	(82.3)	(11.3)	1	-	1	3	5	51 against 49
Orissa100	49	21	70	20						
	(68)	(8)	(76)	(20)						
Bombay200	88	28	116	66	2	-	3	-	13	112 against 88
	(63.1)	(23.7)	(86.8)	(4.4)						
C.P.100	49	34	83	10	1	-	2	2	2	51 against 49
	(71.3)	(15.4)	(88.7)	(7.1)	(3.7)				(3.75)	103 against 49
Madras200	97	45	142	30	14	-	4	2	8	
	(15.1)	(13.5)	(28.6)	(56.5)					(2.1)	63 against 37
Punjab	100	14	13	27	48	1.5	20			2
	(58.1)	(26.4)	(84.5)	(14.8)						
U.P. 100	44	30	74	20	1	-	2	-	3	56 against 44

On Population bases 770 311 1081 344

149 seats less caste Hindus

58 more seats 1 Depressed Classes

i.e. 101 less seats to the Hindus and 99 more seats to Musalmans.

If the Pact of the Minorities would have been arrived at as suggested above, the interest of the Depressed Classes and other Minorities would have been really protected in Separate Electorates and it would have been possible to appoint Muslim, Christian, or Depressed Classes Minister. The interest of the Government would have also been served, because these Ministers would have supported the policy of the British Government in Cabinets. The objection in arriving at such sort of Pact may be taken that as suggested above, Hindus would have got less seats i.e. 149 less than their proportion; the Depressed Classes would have got 38 more seats and the Muslims would have get 99 ninety-nine more seats than their proportions. Just as Dr. Ambedkar has agreed in giving 177 seats more to the Muslims similarly if the Muslims were really sincere and sympathetic towards the uplift of the Depressed Classes, they would have agreed to the suggestion above mentioned and the Depressed Classes would have never condemned the Minorities Pact. But it is the fault of Dr. Ambedkar and not of the Muslims. What principle was adopted in the Pact of the Minorities: arrived at London where by Muslims were given more seats and the Depressed Classes and the Hindus were given less seats than they are entitled to on the population basis? It is evident from the following copy of the context of page 63 of the Minorities Pact.

Annexure

Representation in Legislatures

Figures in Brackets-Population basis 1931 figures and Depressed Classes percentages as per Simon Report.

	Hindu								
	Caste	Depressed Classes	Total	Mus. lims	Chris. tians	Sikh	Anglo Indians	Tribal etc.	Euro peans
Centre All India									
(1931)	(47.5)	(19)*	(66.5)	(21.5)					
Upper 200	101	20	121	67	1	6	1	-	4
Lower 300	123	45	168	100	7	10	3	-	12
*	(48.9)	(13.4)	(62.3)	(34.8)	3	-	1	-	10
Assam 100	38	13	51	35					
	(18.3)	(24.7)	(43)	(54.9)	2	-	3	-	20
Bengal 200	38	35	73	102					
Bihar&	(67.8)	(14.5)	(82.3)	(11.3)	1	-	1	3	5
Orissa 100	51	14	65	25					
	(68)	(8)	(76)	(20)					
Bombay 200	88	28	116	66	2	-	3	-	13
	(63.1)	(23.7)	(86.8)	(4.4)	1	-	2	2	2.7
C.P. 100	58	20	78	15					
	(71.3)	(15.4)	(86.7)	(7.1)	(3.7)				(3.75)
Madras 200	102	40	142	30	14	-	4	2	8
	(13.1)	(13.5)	(28.6)	(56.5)	(13)				(2.1)
Punjab 100	14	10	24	51	1.5	20	1.5	-	2
	(58.1)	(26.4)	(84.4)	(14.8)					(2.4)
U.P. 100	44	20	64	30	1	-	2	-	3

Sind & N.W.F.P Weightage similar to that enjoyed by the Musalmans in the Provincse in which they constitute a minority of the population, shall be given to the Hindu minority in Sind and to the Hindu and Sikh minorities in the N.W.F.P.

According to the above Pact of the Minorities arrived at London; Hindus get 95 less seats and the Depressed Classes get 59 less seats than their proportions while the Muslims get 185 more seats than what they are entitled according to the population basis. On the one hand the Depressed Classes are oppressed by the Hindus and on the other hand their population is decreasing on account of the efforts of the Muslims.

Therefore these Depressed Class Communities with the hope of seeking welfare for they have helped the British Government by being loyal to it. Similarly they believed that they would be helped by the English people at the time of the future reforms. Dr. Ambedkar has agreed 59 less seats; but the Franchise Committees as well as the Provincial Governments of the different Provinces of India have suggested lesser seats than the Minorities Pact of London. The Government may be of opinion that there are no capable and educated persons amongst the Depressed Classes; but this inference is without any basis. It is natural for the Government to feel that there would not be proper candidates for election if the Depressed Classes are given representation on their population basis, because of their experience in the policy of making nominations. But this is not the fault of the Depressed Classes. The C.P. Government has nominated four Depressed Classes Members in the C.P. Legislative Council of whom one does not understand where he is; the other does not understand the proceedings of the Council, because the English language is foreign to him, the third has his mind engaged in other matters except the interest of the Depressed Classes and only the fourth one is real representative of the Depressed Classes. I enclose herewith a copy of the resolutions of which notices were given by the Depressed Classes nominated members of the C.P. Legislative Council. In this Province there are about 100 persons of the Depressed Classes who can understand the significance and the importance of the Council and the position of the other provinces in this respect is the same. Bengal and Madras - these two Provinces are far advanced in the education of the Depressed Classes. After being convinced that the Depressed Classes are not going to have proportionate representation, the All India Depressed Classes Association has made a Pact with the All India Hindu Mahasabha at Delhi. According to this Pact the Depressed Classes are entitled to seats in all the Legislatures as follows:-

Upper Chamber	38
Lower Chamber	57
Assam	13
Bengal	49
Bihar & Orissa	14
Bombay	16
Central Provinces	24
Madras	30
Punjab	13
U.P.	26

Before this Pact of Delhi was arrived at, the consent of the Members of the Working Committee of the All India Depressed Classes Association as well as of other Depressed Classes Leaders was obtained. But Dr. Ambedkar has taken the consent of no other person except Rao Bahadur Shrinivasan. It is said that Dr. Ambedkar got the support of the whole Depressed Classes when he was in London. I admit this in some respect. I also supported him. The chief reason for the support of the Depressed Classes at the second session of the Round Table Conference to Dr. Ambedkar was, for his changed policy. He made a speech in the first session of the Round Table conference to the effect that the English people and the British Government have done nothing for the welfare of these classes and the English people are timid. And in the second Round Table Conference he fought with Mr. Gandhi without criticising the policy of the British Government. This made him to get support of the Depressed Classes. Why did he not get the support in the first Round Table Conference? While supporting Dr. Ambedkar in the Second Round Table Conference, the Depressed Classes did not support the Minorities Pact and have always claimed for representation on the population basis. While arriving at the Minorities Pact the Musalmans have taken 185 more seat and gave 59 seats less to these Classes. The Provincial Governments in their recommendations to the Indian Franchise Committee have suggested lesser seats than this Pact of London for the Depressed Classes. These Classes therefore were disappointed in both these ways. Naturally we had to join the Hindus whose majority will be formed in the future Provincial Autonomy in most of the Legislatures. They (Hindus) accepted our condition of representation on the population basis with reserved seats and we have accepted their condition of Joint Electorates. I have made it clear in my first statement of the 31st March 1932; a copy of which is enclosed herewith that it is not possible to have elected the Depressed Classes who would always be under the influence of the Hindus. It is also made clear in the Report of the Simon Commission (Volume 2 Page 65) that the blot of untouchability of the Depressed Classes can only be removed in Joint Electorates and so the Commission has recommended joint electorates with reserved seats for these Classes, but in order to guard against being elected the Depressed Classes who may be the underlings of the Hindus; the Commission has suggested in the same Report on the next Page 66 that the Governor should be given power to certify which candidates are authorised to stand for the Depressed Classes seats after consultation with the Depressed Classes Associations. This portion of the recommendation of the Commission was condemned by the Depressed Classes as it is just like the present system of making Nominations.

Dr. Ambedkar's Changing Policy

I had indicated on the 28th May 1930 in my letter to their Excellencies the Governors of the different Provinces and His Excellency the Viceroy and the Right Honourable the State Secretary for India that it was published in Indian News Papers that Dr. Ambedkar had supported the revolutionary move of Mr. Gandhi. I now feel that my writing in the letter proved true in reference to the speech made by him at the 1st Round Table Conference. In that Report of the 12th November 1930 - 19th January 1931, Dr. Ambedkar in his speech says as follows:- (Page 123-129 first Report of the R.T.C.) "When we compare our present position with the one which it was our lot to bear in Indian society of the pre British days we find that instead of marching on, we are only marking time. Before the British, we were in loathsome condition due to our untouchability. Has the British Government done anything to remove it? Before the British, we could not draw water from the village well. Has the British Government secured us the right to the well? Before the British, we could not enter the temple. Can we enter now? Before the British, we were denied entry into the Police Force. Does the British Government admit us in the Force? Before the British, we were not allowed to serve in the Military. Is that career now open to us?

We do not accuse the British of indifference or want of sympathy. What we find is that they are quite incompetent to tackle our problem.

It is not because they cannot help us in these things but because it is against their character, motives and interest to do so. The second consideration that limits its authority is the mortal fear it has of external resistance.

The Government of India does realize that the landlords are squeezing the masses dry, and the capitalists are not giving the labourers a living wage and decent condition of work. Yet it is most painful thing that it has not dared to touch any of these evils. Why? Is it because it has no legal powers to remove them? No. The reason why it does not intervene is because it is afraid that its intervention to amend the existing code of social and economic life, will give rise to resistance. Of what good is such a Government to anybody?

"This role the British Government will never be able to play. It is only a government which is of the people for the people and by the people that will make this possible.

"No share of this political power can evidently come to us so long as the British Government remains as it is. In only a Swaraj constitution that we stand any chance of getting the political power into our own hands without which we can not bring salvation to our people.

"The Depressed Classes have had no friend. The Government has all along used them only as an excuse for its continued existence. The Hindus claim them only to deny them or, better still, to appropriate, their rights. The Mahomedans refuse to recognize their separate existence because they fear that their privileges may be curtailed by the admission of a rival. Depressed by the Government, suppressed by the Hindus and disregarded by the Muslim etc.

I am afraid it is not sufficiently realised that in the present temper of the country; no constitution will be workable which is not acceptable to the majority of the people. The time when you were to choose and India was to accept is gone, never to return."

Dr. Ambedkar's presidential address at the All India Depressed Classes Congress, First Session, Nagpur: Friday and Saturday. August 8 and 9, 1930 was made on the same lines of his speech at the first Round Table Conference.

After his speech in 1930 he has changed his views at the Second Round Table Conference and his changing in policy depends upon his will. He may change his present views in 1933.

Dr. Ambedkar's All India Depressed Classes Kamptee Congress

(His Congress had been dissolved in Kamptee and he has started a new body a Federation!)

Dr. Ambedkar's Congress recently held at Kamptee proved futile. It was to be held in March 1932 and after that they fixed 24th & 25th April 32 for the Congress. 30th April and 1st May 32 was also announced a third time for holding the Congress but it was held on the 7th & 8th May 32. Besides this, it is held in a village in a corner. In the name of the All India Depressed Classes Congress only 1500 persons from

Nagpur and Kamptee were gathered including 4 or 5 delegates from out side. They have published that the representatives of the All India Depressed Classes Association we were invited to attend the Congress but that is all false. None of the representatives of our Association was invited for the Congress. Such sort of Congress cannot be an All India Depressed Classes Congress.

All India Depressed Classes Association

There have been 9 nine Annual Sessions of the All India Depressed Classes Conference at principal Cities like Nagpur, Delhi, Madras, Allahabad, Meerut, Amraoti, Gudhgaon and others and hundreds of Provincial—and District Conferences were held under the auspices of the All India Depressed Classes Association. The 10th annual session is to be held at Bombay where Dr. Ambedkar lives, this year in June 1932. This Association was founded by me and Mr. Gavai. The Members of this Association have never changed like Dr. Ambedkar in respect of the policy of the British Government. We claim Joint electorates not for the interests of the Hindus but for the interests of the Depressed Classes. If the Government had given us hopes for our representation on population basis, this controversy would never have arisen.

I as the Vice President of the Registered All India Jati Sudhar Maha Sabha, as a Member of the Executive Committee of the Registered Depressed India Association and as the Asstt. General Secretary of the All India Association and as the Secretary of the C.P. & Berar Depressed Classes Education Society, humbly pray to His Majesty's Government to grant Joint Electorates with reservation of seats on the population basis for the Depressed Classes. It will be for the benefit both of the British Government and of the Depressed Classes.

Nagpur

3.6.32

G.M. Thaware

Asstt. General Secretary

All India Depressed Classes Association

**

7. P.N. Rajahbhoj
President,
207 Ghorpade Peth, Poona 2
Provincial All India Depressed Classes Association
Member Poona City Municipality.
District Local Board Poona
Editor:- Dalit Bandhu

Dated
7th June 1932

To,

The Private Secretary
to his Excellency the Viceroy and
Governor General of India, Simla.

Sir,

We beg leave to request you to kindly place the following representation before His Excellency the Viceroy and Governor General of India for his kind consideration.

We, the representatives of the Depressed Classes in general and of the Chamar and Mang communities in particular, hereby declare that we do not recognize Dr. Ambedkar and his co-worker from Madras as the leaders of Depressed communities all over India in so far as they advocate separate electorates for these communities. Only a few months ago, Dr. Ambedkar declared from the platform and through the press his opposition to such electorates at various centres of public opinion. His selection for the membership of the R.T.C. brought about a great change in his opinion and the metamorphosis was so complete and so sudden that it fairly startled all his friends, admirers and followers, most of whom are still abiding by the decision that educated Depressed opinion took in the matter of representation in the future legislatures. We confess that we cannot diagnose this sudden change; but perfectly well acquainted as we are with the trend of thought in our communities, we can say without fear of contradiction that Dr. Ambedkar and his co-worker on the R.T.C. have done a positive disservice to the community which they profess to represent in that they have by the peculiar line of thinking they have adopted, perhaps unconsciously, torn the Depressed communities from the bulk of the Hindu population.

Separate electorate is a curse from first to last. This institution once established will alienate the sympathies of the Hindu communities and our representatives in the Council will always join hands with the Mussalmans between whom and the Hindus in general there is little love lost. The more they side with them and the oftener they work against the interest of the Hindus in this strange company, the wider will be the gulf that already spreads between the Depressed and the touchables. All our social movements are without doubt based upon the fundamental assumption that we are Hindus, that we mean to remain Hindus and that if there is any fight between us, it is entirely the business of the so called Untouchables and Touchables. Once under the baneful influence of Muslim neighbourhood in the Council, Depressed communities drift farther away, the very bottom of future unification of these two races, for which the advanced thought in both camps is striving, shall have been knocked out; and out of sheer helplessness, the Depressed communities will be gradually delivered into the hands of the Mussalmans, whose friendship, from experience we know, is more harmful than is the patent indifference of the high-class Hindus.

It is contended that the Councils will work only for the political uplift of our communities and that, therefore, their social relations with the bulk of the Hindus may not undergo a change for the worse. But all this is pure pretence. For, has not Dr. Ambedkar time and again said that he wants political power for social redemption and do we not know how, with the political weapons thus framed, aggressive communities are making social encroachment on others? If this is true, then the talk of keeping our political power and our social re-adjustments aloof from each other is all balderdash.

Communities other than the Mahars have never expressed their allegiance to the leadership of Dr. Ambedkar—communities whose voice has till now failed to be heard in responsible quarters. If Dr. Ambedkar fears that our interests would certainly suffer, if he casts in his own lot with the other Hindus, then we have our own fears regarding the treatment that some of us, who are the Depressed within the Depressed, may get at his hands. We are frank and we say that we are exceedingly nervous on this point, and that not without reason. In fact, an attempt was made to begin discussions in the matter of a private understanding for a mutual adjustment and apportionment of political power that a united front might win at the R.T.C. But Dr. Ambedkar would not even deign to look to the proposals sought to be placed before him by the representatives of smaller Depressed communities, who are more ill at ease when in the company of his community than in that of the higher classes. Our position would be not at all an enviable one. We, therefore, oppose the principle of separate electorates with all the emphasis at our command and thoroughly endorse the policy that our veteran leader Rao Bahadur Rajah from Madras has adopted.

This policy of opposition to separate and advocacy of joint electorates was endorsed by a resolution at the All India Depressed Classes Conference held recently at Kamptee, and it remains the policy favoured by a large majority of the members of Depressed Classes.

Finally we must state in all sincerity that we bear no ill will to Dr. Ambedkar. Indeed we are conscious that the Depressed Classes owe much to him for their present awakening. But we cannot lend our support to separate electorates favoured by him and that is our sole ground of opposition to him. This opposition is even misrepresented in certain quarters as opposition to Government, but the fact is that the Depressed Classes, whatever their views on the method of representation, are passionately loyal to the British Government, and in this respect no discrimination can be made with any show of reason in favour of Dr. Ambedkar's followers and against us, the supporters of joint electorates.

We beg to remain,

Sir,

Your most obedient and humble servants,

Sd. P.N. Rajabhoj

A. J. Sonone B.A.

P.K. Shivdas

**

8. From

J.M. Clay Esqr., C.I.E., O.B.E., I.C.S.,
Chief Secretary to Government,
United Provinces.

To

The Reforms Officer,
Government of India,
Home Department,
Simla

Dated Naini Tal, August 10, 1932

Sir,

I am directed to forward herewith copies of certain resolutions passed at the two conferences of the depressed classes at Gorakhpur and Etawah respectively for the information of the Government of India and such action, if any, as may be deemed necessary.

I have the honour to be,
Sir,
Your most obedient servant,
J.M. Clay
Chief Secretary

No action is required on this. It will be placed on the Depressed Classes file.

W H Lewis
15.8.32

Copy of resolutions passed at a Conference of the U.P. Depressed Classes Association on July 9&10, 1932.

Resolution No. 1. That this conference does not see any cause for complaint in the procedure announced by the Secretary of State on the 27th of June 1932, and fully approves of it as this is the only method by which the outstanding problems can satisfactorily be solved consistently with the expedition urged by the Indian Public opinion.

Resolution No. 2. Whereas Dr. B.R. Ambedkar and Rao Bahadur S. Srinivasan, the only 2 representatives of the depressed classes at the R.T.C.. and its Committees especially the Indian Franchise Committee, are wholly unaware of the real nature of the problem of depressed classes in U.P., the case of these classes has practically been judged ex parte and has not received the consideration it deserves, and whereas no representatives of depressed classes of U.P., in fact of the whole of northern India was appointed on the R.T.C. and its committees, therefore it is resolved that H.E. The Viceroy be moved to receive a deputation consisting of the following gentlemen with a view to make out their case for the urgent necessity of giving adequate representation to the depressed classes of these Provinces, on the R.T.C. or its substitute, the Consultative Committee:-

1. Rai Saheb Baboo Ram Charan B.A. LL.B Advocate M.L.C. Lucknow
2. Baboo Ram Das Jiwit, Benares.
3. Baboo Mahabir Prasad, Cawnpore.
4. Swami Kshama Nand, Etawah.
5. Baboo Mathura Prasad, Gorakhpur.

Resolution No. 3. Resolved that it is the considered opinion of this conference that the definition of Depressed classes framed by the Indian Franchise Committee is unduly narrow, rather unreal as observed by H.E. Sir Malcolm Hailey on the 7th of June 1932 in reply to an address presented by the depressed classes of Almora, and Dr. Ambedkar's concurrence to it in the Indian Franchise Committee is only due to his ignorance of the real condition of depressed classes in Northern India, this conference strongly urges the Rt. Hon'ble Mr. Ramsay Mac Donald, the Premier of England and through him His Majesty's Government that at least both the classes designated as 'Backward' and 'Depressed' by the Hon'ble Mr. E.A.H. Blunt, Finance Member U.P. Government. be accepted as forming the depressed classes of these provinces, otherwise classes wrongly designated as 'Backward' classes' which have all along been treated as depressed classes by the Government and by all concerned, are bound to go unrepresented, all the extension of franchise not-withstanding.

Resolution No. 4. Whereas the problem of depressed classes in the U.P. and for the matter of that in the whole of Northern India is so dissimilar to that obtaining in Southern India, the only useful method of representation for these classes is the one recommended by the Indian Statutory Commission, therefore this conference wholly supports joint electorates with reservation of seats embodied in what is known as the Rajah-Moonje Pact for the whole of India.

Copy Of Resolutions Passed At A Meeting Of The Depressed Classes At Gorakhpur On June 29, 1932.

3. This Conference desires to make it plain that the Depressed Classes claim special representation as a matter of natural rights necessary for their protection.

4. This conference most emphatically repudiates the so-called Rajah-Moonje Pact as it is highly detrimental to the interest of the Depressed Classes of India.

5. This conference very much appreciates the most magnificent services rendered by Dr. B.R. Ambedkar and Rao Bahadur Shrinivasan for the Depressed Classes at the Indian Round Table Conference and expresses its full confidence in them.

6. To secure for the depressed classes the right of representation through separate electorates in all local bodies in proportion to their population.

**

*Source N. A. I.: File 111/32-R

Section III
Newspaper Reports

9. The Free Press Journal
Bombay
17-10-1931

HOLLOW THUNDER OF DR. AMBEDKAR

When Did He Wake Up?

Disabilities Nearer Home

What Has He Done About Them?

A FEW POINTERS

To the Editor of "Free Press Journal": —

Sir,

Before the arrival in India of the unwelcome and largely boycotted Simon Commission Dr. Ambedkar was quite a nonentity, so much so, that outside the student world of the Law College not a soul knew that there existed in the city of Bombay a person of the blessed name of Dr. Ambedkar. One would like in all seriousness to ask where has Dr. Ambedkar been all these years. What has he been doing to ameliorate the unhappy conditions of the unfortunate Untouchables? Did he have a hand in opening Seminaries for them, if not, did he at least co-operate wholeheartedly with those who have been conducting them. Is he aware of the most disgraceful fact that in the suburbs and far away places in the mofussil how in past public conveyances used to refuse to carry members of the untouchable classes from ports and railway stations to their destination in the interior?

Is Dr. Ambedkar aware of another most disgraceful fact that such of the untouchables as cremate their dead are driven to carry the dead to such a far off place as Sewri by reason of the most indignant and tyrannical refusal of the Un-Aryan Hindu Burning Ground Committee to let them cremate their dead at the most centrally situated burning near Marine Lines known as *Sonapur?*

Has Dr. Ambedkar attempted through any rich man to have a temple built in the same way as Barrister Sawarkar has done in Ratnagiri.

What is the good of his thundering forth that he is the stoutest champion of the untouchables when there are no deeds to his credit to back his declaration? The absence of any action belies his audacious statement. What are Dr. Ambedkar's credentials to sit in judgment upon Mahatmaji and to question his *bona fides* to speak for the Depressed Classes? Is he aware of the universally known truth that Mahatmaji has made abolition of untouchability his religion? To doubt the sincerity of one who has espoused the cause of the untouchables as no other individual within living memory has done or to call him names is like spitting at the sun whose powerful rays are too strong for the poor vision of the misguided Doctor. He has thereby exposed himself to the ridicule of the whole universe.

Yours faithfully,
(Sd.) S. V. JAYAKAR
Lohar Ali, Chendni, Thana

**

10. The Bombay Chronicle

Bombay

21-10-1931

"We have full faith In Mahatma"

MASS MEETING OF "UNTOUCHABLES" OF BOMBAY

Dr. Ambedkar Disowned

Hundreds of members of the "Depressed" Classes of Bombay and the suburbs were present at a meeting held at Lower Parel on Tuesday morning under the presidentship of Mr. Sakharam Buwa. The meeting passed a resolution expressing full confidence in Mahatma Gandhi and repudiating Dr. Ambedkar's claim to represent all the "Depressed" Classes.

The resolution which was moved by Mr. B. J. Deorukhkar disapproved of separate electorates and demanded joint electorates and adult suffrage and approved of Mahatma Gandhi's suggestion in favour of co-operation.

The resolution was carried unanimously and great enthusiasm prevailed throughout.

Mr. Sakharam Buwa Kajrolkar, a well-known dramatist and leader of the so-called Depressed Classes said that they had met here to support Mahatmaji. "You know that Mahatma Gandhi is doing his best to remove the blot of Untouchability from Hinduism. He has great love for the Untouchables. Our friend Dr. Ambedkar who has been nominated by the Government to represent us has also some wonderful scheme and he has also put up his scheme before R. T. C. These schemes of Dr. Ambedkar are changing as the Doctor has also undergone a wonderful change in his outlook and has found strange bedfellows in Maulana Shaukat Ali and other reactionaries.

Ambedkar of Pre-R.T.C. Days

At Nagpur Congress of the Depressed Classes he told them that he didn't want Separate Electorates. He wanted joint electorates but with some conditions. One of his chief conditions was there should be Adult Suffrage and some reservation for a little time. Mahatma Gandhi on behalf of the Congress has agreed to Adult Suffrage but now the Doctor wants Separate Electorates.

Doctor Disowned

Continuing Mr. Sakharam Buwa said that the worthy Doctor who is chaperoned in London by "Big Brother" and the Aga Khan and other Muslim communalist leaders in the absence of any arguments for separate electorates takes delight in abusing Gandhiji and the Congress leaders. It was very regrettable that the Doctor does all this dirty mudslinging in the name of the "Untouchables" of the country. "We hereby disown Dr. Ambedkar and repudiate his claim to represent the whole community. We affirm our faith in Mahatma and pray that his mission to London in the cause of the country and the Congress may be crowned with success.

Mr. Sakharam Buwa then called upon Mr. Deorukhkar to move the resolution.

Mr. Deorukhkar then put before the meeting a resolution which expressed full confidence in Mahatma Gandhi and repudiated Dr. Ambedkar's claim to represent the Depressed Classes, as he was only a nominee of the Government.

The resolution further disapproved of Separate Electorates and demanded Joint Electorates and adult suffrage and approved of Mahatma Gandhi's suggestion of co-option. The resolution, however, stated that if reservation of seats were given then in that case each section among the Depressed Classes should be given adequate representation.

Mr. Deorukhkar said that the resolution by itself did not require any elaboration for the heart of the Depressed Classes was sound. But what he wanted to tell his comrades was that Dr. Ambedkar was definitely now playing into the hands of the British Imperialists and Indian reactionaries. As such he had no right to speak on behalf of the entire Depressed Classes. The very fact that as soon as the Doctor's effusions in London were known in India all over the country meetings have been held by the Depressed Classes repudiating him and reaffirming their faith in the Mahatma shows which way the wind was blowing. Dr. Ambedkar by his mud-slinging at Gandhiji and his cheap gibes at the Congressmen might delight the British Imperialists and his new found friends in the "Big Brother" and the Aga Khan but shall carry no weight either with his own compatriots here or with real honest politicians in England.

Dr. Ambedkar's insistence on Separate Electorates for the Depressed Classes was mischievous and anti-national. Whatever might be the past mistakes and sins of commission and omission by their high class Hindu brethren times were fast changing. The Congress and Mahatma had times out of number expressed their determination to wipe out this blot of untouchability and it was no use merely perpetuating the class hatred by demanding separate electorates, which were a hindrance in the progress towards full blooded nationalism.

Dr. Ambedkar could not try to monopolise the leadership of the entire Depressed Classes. Better and more tried leaders of their community had always shown a compromising spirit. Leaders like Mr. P. Baloo and other influential men from their own classes had explained to them before this that the Depressed Classes had nothing to fear from joint electorates. Mahatma Gandhi before his departure had consultations with Mr. P. Baloo and other members of the Depressed Classes and it was foolish to imagine that Mahatma does not know where the interests of the classes lie.

The part played by the Depressed Classes in the city of Bombay and outside in the last Civil Disobedience movement was a proof positive of the backing of this class to the Congress cause. A number of the Depressed Classes members went to jail and bore *lathi charges* under the Congress flag. It was this common bond of suffering and sacrifice in the cause of motherland that was gone to wipe out the old feuds and past sins.

As one representing the younger section of the depressed classes Mr. Deorukhkar made a declaration that in case the Congress was forced to start the Civil Disobedience movement the Depressed Classes would not lag behind in giving their quota of men to the country.

The resolution was unanimously carried amidst shouts of "Mahatma Gandhi-ki-jai" and "Inquilab Zindabad". Messrs. Shankarrao Chandodkar, (city father, Kurla) Deolekar, Pendarkar, Shingarpurkar, Vithal Patankar, Gopal Konvindkar and Mr. Krishna Sadashiv Deo addressed the gathering. Another resolution was passed at the meeting giving support to the Guryaur (Kerala) Temple entry *satyagrah.*

**

11. The Bombay Chronicle

Bombay

2-12-1931

DR. AMBEDKAR IN ANTI-SWARAJIST ROLE

Mr. Mohanlal, Secretary, Punjab "*Achhut-Uddhar" Mandal,* writes:—

"Consistency as a virtue is seldom to be found among our present-day politicians. Dr. Ambedkar, "representing" the Depressed Classes at the Round Table Conference, is no exception to this common type of politicians. He has now turned an *anti-Swarajist* because his views regarding the representation of the Depressed Classes in the *Swaraj* constitution could not find acceptance with Mahatma Gandhi. In the course of his speech at the Minorities Sub-Committee he is reported to have made the following observations:

"Dr. Ambedkar desired to make it clear that the Depressed Classes had not started any movement for claiming immediate transfer of power from the British to the Indian people. They had their particular grievances against the British people, but they were not clamouring for transfer of political power. Their position was that they were not anxious for it."

These are Dr. Ambedkar's view in the blessed year of 1931. But such were not his ideas when he presided at the Nagpur sessions of the All-India Depressed Classes Conference last year. Addressing his hearers in the course of his presidential speech, he observed:—

"Before the British you were in a loathsome condition due to your Untouchability." What has British Government done to remove your "Untouchability"? Before the British Government you could not draw water from the village wells. Has the British Government secured you the right to the well? Before the British you could not enter the temple. Can you enter now? Before the British you were denied the entry into the police force. Does the British Government admit you in the force? Before the British you were not allowed to serve in the Military. Is that career now open to you? Gentlemen, to none of these questions, you can give an affirmative answer. Your wrongs have remained as open sores and they have not been righted and I say that the British Government, actuated by the best of motives and principles, will always remain powerless to effect any change. Nobody can remove your grievances as well as you can and you cannot remove these unless you get political power in your hands. No share of political power can come to you so long as the British Government remains where it is."

How can these grievances of the downtrodden untouchables be removed? says Dr. Ambedkar in the same speech:

We must have a Government in which men in power will give undivided allegiance to the best interests of the country. We must have a Government in which men in power, knowing where obedience will end and resistance will begin, will not be afraid to amend the social and economic code of life which the dictates of justice and expediency so urgently call for. This role the British Government will never be able to play. It is only a Government which is of the people, for the people and by the people, in other words, it is only the *Swaraj* Government that will make it possible.

In the face of this emphatic pronouncement in favour of *Swaraj* by Dr. Ambedkar himself, as President of the All-India Depressed Classes' Conference in 1930, is it not sheer audacity on his part to say at the Minority Sub-Committee that the Depressed Classes are not clamouring for *Swaraj?* Surely, there must be a limit to inconsistencies beyond which it is dangerous for a responsible politician of the type of Dr. Ambedkar to tread.

**

12. The Bombay Chronicle

Bombay

23-2-1932

LOTHIAN COMMITTEE — COMES PREPARED

Took Decision For Separate Electorates For Depressed Classes Before Starting

Dr. Ambedkar's Propaganda Methods

Propaganda of a very abject nature has been instituted by Dr. Ambedkar since his return from England to manufacture opinion among the Depressed Classes in favour of Separate Electorates.

Dr. Ambedkar, just before he left for the first Session of the Round Table Conference, presiding over Depressed Classes Conference at Nagpur emphasised that Joint Electorates with reserved seats were in the best interests of his community. In his famous minute of dissent to the Bombay Provincial Simon Committee report also he declared that communal electorates were the greatest evil, responsible for the growth of communal rivalry and tension in India. Joint Electorates alone with reserved seat would serve his community best.

Changed Beyond Recognition

But the two London trips that he made during 1930 and 1931 as a member of the Round Table Conference and the St. James Palace atmosphere in which he lived changed him beyond recognition. When he returned he came as a champion of Separate Electorates. He has prepared a set of answers to the questionnaire issued by the Franchise Committee and copies of the same are being circulated among various individual members and mushroom associations of the Depressed Classes community. Space has been left at the beginning of every paragraph to fill up the blanks with the names of the Association, or individuals,

Stereotyped Replies

The hundreds of the Stereotyped replies to the questionnaire circulated repeat.

"The ... (the blank space is to be filled up by the name of the Association) is of opinion that the Depressed Classes cannot secure representation in the general electorates. Much less can they secure representatives of their own choice. Even if there was adult suffrage. The reasons are as follows:-

"*(a)* In every territorial constituency the Depressed Classes are in minority of the population and will be a minority of voters in the electorate much too small to win a seat for themselves.

"*(b)* Owing to social prejudices no voter of the higher caste will vote for the Depressed Classes candidates.

"*c)* On the other hand owing to economic dependence on the higher castes and the religious and social influence of the higher classes voters may be led to vote for a high caste candidate as against a candidate of his own Class. No Depressed Class man has ever been elected to the Council on the support of high castes."

Already Decided

Questions were put to Dr. Ambedkar by some of the members of the Depressed Classes whether Separate Electorates would not perpetuate untouchability instead of removing the community's disabilities. Dr. Ambedkar with a tinge of bureaucracy replied that the declaration of the political rights of the community in the fundamental rights clause would remove the disabilities. Law would make it impossible for any member of any so-called higher class communities to treat his community as " Untouchables".

Effectively to check the growth of any opinion in favour of joint electorates in his community, he is reported to have disclosed that travelling as he did, with the members of the Franchise Committee by S. S. "Mooltan" last month.

The Committee had come with definite instructions and pre-conceived decision to recommend separate electorate for the minority communities and that any amount of support for joint electorates would not improve matters. His community, as practical people, should no longer waste time in preparing cases for joint electorates but get ready to work a constitution based on separate electorates.

In order to consolidate the position of his community, Dr. Ambedkar is aiming to form an All-India Board — an organisation parallel to the Indian National Congress composed of the various 46 sub-sections of the Depressed Class.

These 46 sub-sections constitute what the Start Committee called "Untouchability within Untouchability". For example, Chammars consider that Mahars rank lower to their status and position in society. They do not inter-dine and inter-marry. Chammars will not use the wells used by Mahars. Excepting the common factor that all of them are called Hindus, their social customs, manners and culture are different from one another.

All the 46 sub-sections of the Depressed Classes will be represented on the proposed board which will select and run candidates for the elections issuing one manifesto. Elected members will enter into, vote and act in the legislatures as a party and form ministries also in co-operation with other parties in the legislatures. But what the "Baba Sahib" as Dr. Ambedkar is called by his supporters, is unable to find a solution for is how to distribute among the various sub-sections the fewer seats that he may be allocated for his community in any legislature. Dr. Ambedkar is assuring every sub-sections of adequate representation and in certain cases is prepared to concede "Separate Electorates within Separate Electorates". He is still working at the problems and the solution will be read with great interest when he publishes the same.

**

13. The Statesman

Delhi

24-2-1932

Congress Policy Condemned

Untouchables' View

Joint Electorate Asked At Delhi Meeting

Condemnation of Congress opposition to the group system and indirect election, and a plea for a joint electorate with reservation of seats, were features of the meeting yesterday of the Working Committee of the All-India Depressed Classes Association, which met under the presidency of Rao Bahadur M.C. Rajah, M.L.A.

The following resolutions were adopted unanimously:-

The Working Committee of the All-India Depressed Classes Association humbly pays its homage of loyalty to the British Throne and prays that the King-Emperor and the Royal Family may long rule over us so that through them the British ideals of justice, freedom and progress may be established in India.

The Working Committee emphatically condemns all attempts to prevent co-operation of the people of this country with the Government and expresses its strong convictions that the progress of the country can be achieved only through hearty and intelligent co-operation with the British Government.

Fundamental Rights

The Working Committee, while condemning the attempted outrage on the Governor of Bengal, congratulates His Excellency on his providential escape.

It is of the utmost importance that fundamental rights should be embodied in the new constitution of India; instead of the term Depressed Classes the term Adi-Hindu should be used in drafting the new constitution. The provincial Governments should prepare lists of "untouchable" classes and these lists should be embodied in the rules under the electoral rules of each and every province; seats should be allocated to the community in the legislatures on a population basis and the Committee do not agree with the Minority Pact with reference to the number of seats fixed for Bengal, Central Provinces, Punjab and United Provinces.

Wider Franchise

The Committee also resolved that the present franchise qualifications should be lowered and the electorate enlarged, as suggested by the Indian

Statutory Commission, to secure the same proportion of voters to the population in different communities; direct elections will benefit the community and the Committee rejects the proposal of the group system and indirect voting; literacy and education, primary school leaving certificate should also be considered as a qualification independently of property.

In view of the impending rapid changes in the Government of this country and in view of the statement by the Prime Minister to the Round Table Conference at the close of its second session on December 1, 1931, that provincial autonomy will be given to provinces, the Working Committee is of the opinion that reservation of seats in joint electorates will be highly beneficial for returning members of the community to the Legislatures; out of the number of seats earmarked for the community for the Lower House of the Federal Legislature one seat should be given to the Depressed Classes of Delhi province.

**

14. The Bombay Chronicle
Bombay
27-2-1932

DR. AMBEDKAR'S FUTILE THREAT

"Breach Between Us And War Amongst Ourselves"

Those Threatening Letters and Model Answers

Moonje- Rajah Pact and After

(From Our Special Correspondent)

New Delhi, February 26

The threat of "breach between us and war amongst ourselves" by Dr. Ambedkar and protest to Lord Lothian against this intimidation by one of the members of his Committee are the latest developments that have come to light in connection with the decision of the All-India Depressed Classes Association to stand for joint-electorates with reservation of seats.

It seems that on finding that the President of the association had made a declaration in favour of joint electorate and fearing the association might endorse it thereby disowning all his activities in London, Dr. Ambedkar wrote the following letter to Mr. G. A. Gavai, M.L.C., General Secretary, All-India Depressed Classes Association and members of C. P. Provincial Franchise Committee:

Ambedkar Perturbed

I am sending you a copy of the memorandum containing my views which I am sending you for your information. You will notice from the last para in the memorandum that our Committee cannot and therefore your Committee cannot discuss communal question. The Prime Minister's letter and questionnaire issued by the Committee makes this clear and the Chairman of our Committee has given a ruling on this question both at Delhi and Lucknow which has been in accord with this view. Therefore you must tell your Committee that they cannot discuss this question and if they insist, you should refuse to discuss it. Your separate minute, instead of discussing joint 'versus' separate electorates should simply say that you refuse to discuss it, because it is outside the terms of reference of the Committee. I know your association has got a questionnaire.

Shocked at Rajah's Attitude

There is just one thing I must point out. I was shocked to find out that Mr. Rajah has changed his opinion and is now advocating joint electorates. I hope your association will not follow him in this policy which is suicidal in every way, but if it does, then you must take the consequences of a permanent breach between us and a war against ourselves which I am trying to avoid at any cost. So don't persist in it. I am glad to have the assurance that you won't do anything without my knowledge and consent. I have written out a detailed set of answers to the Franchise Committee questionnaire. I will send you a copy as soon as they are typed.

Futile Threat

It is well known that this threat did not succeed in intimidating those who upheld joint-electorate with reservation of seats on population basis and the conclusion of a pact between them and the all India Hindu Maha Sabha already marks the successful conclusion of this healthy development.

Threatening Letters

The protest lodged with Lord Lothian against a member of the Committee sending threatening letters and model answers may or may not have its effect but the Working Committee of the Association holds that the questionnaire issued by the Lothian Committee gave Depressed Classes a special place and invited, in respect of these classes, opinion as to whether there should be separate or joint electorates for them and on what proportion.

Misleading Information

Mr. Gavai has taken an early opportunity to issue the following statement to members of Depressed Classes. "Certain misleading information is being circulated to you that the Indian Franchise Committee cannot discuss the question of the system of electorates with individuals or associations that submit memoranda to it on behalf of the Depressed Classes. This is very misleading. For in the questionnaire sent by the Committee under the item representation of Depressed Classes in paper 2, it is clearly stated what specific proposals would one make to secure representation of the community in the legislature.

Those Model Answers

Moreover, I would suggest that our associations would be well advised to send in their own views with reference to their own provinces irrespective of model answers prepared by others. In view of coming changes in the Constitution of India as declared by the Prime Minister on 1st of December 1931 that complete provincial autonomy will be given to provinces. It is very necessary that our community should also keep pace with the times and so we should reconsider the decision which we had arrived at before the statement of the Prime Minister referred to above.

**

15. The Leader
Allahabad
28-2-1932

Joint Electorates
Dr. Ambedkar on War Path
A Threat That Failed
Protest to Lord Lothian

(From Our Correspondent)

New Delhi, Feb. 26

A threat of 'breach between us and war amongst ourselves' by Dr. Ambedkar and a protest to Lord Lothian against this intimidation by one of the members of his committee are the latest developments that have come to light in connection with the decision of the All-India Depressed Classes Association to stand for joint electorates with reservation of seats. It seems that on finding that the president of the Association had made a declaration in favour of joint electorate and fearing that the Association might endorse it thereby disowning all his activities in London, Dr. Ambedkar wrote the following to Mr. G.A. Gavai, M.L.C., general secretary of the All-India Depressed Classes Association and member of the C.P. Provincial Franchise Committee:-

'I am sending you a copy of a memorandum containing my views which I am sending you for your information. You will notice from the last para in the memorandum that our committee cannot and, therefore, your committee cannot discuss the communal question. The Prime Minister's letter and the questionnaire issued by the committee makes this clear and the chairman of our committee has given a ruling on this question both at Delhi and Lucknow, which is in accord with this view. Therefore, you must tell your committee that they cannot discuss this question and if they insist you should refuse to discuss it. Your separate minute instead of discussing joint *versus* separate electorates should simply say that you refuse to discuss it because it is outside the terms of the committee. I know your Association has got a questionnaire. There is just one thing I must point out. I was shocked to find out that Mr. Rajah has changed his opinion and is now advocating joint electorates. I hope your Association will not follow him in this policy which is suicidal in every way, but if it does, then you must take the consequences of a permanent breach between us and a war amongst ourselves which I am trying to avoid at any cost. So don't persist in it. I am glad to have the assurance that you won't do anything without my knowledge and consent.

I have written out a detailed set of answers to the Franchise Committee questionnaire. I will send you a copy as soon as they are typed.'

It is well-known that this did not succeed in intimidating the working committee of the All-India Depressed Classes Association who upheld the joint electorate with reservation of seats on a population basis and the conclusion of a pact between them and the All-India Hindu Mahasabha already marks the successful conclusion of this healthy development. The protest lodged with Lord Lothian against a member of the committee sending threatening letters and model answers may or may not have its effect but the working committee of the Association holds that the questionnaire issued by the Lothian Committee gave the depressed classes a special place and invited in respect of these classes opinion as to whether there should be separate or joint electorates for them and in what proportion. Mr. Gavai has taken an early opportunity to issue the following statement to the members of the depressed classes:- 'Certain misleading information is being circulated to you that the Indian Franchise Committee cannot discuss the question of system of electorates with individuals or associations that submit memoranda to it on behalf of the depressed classes. This is very misleading, for in the questionnaire sent by the committee under the item 'representation of depressed classes' in para 2 it is clearly asked what proposals one would make to secure a representative of the community in the legislature. Moreover, I would suggest that our associations should be well advised to send in their own views with reference to their own provinces irrespective of model answers prepared by others. In view of the coming changes in the constitution of India as declared by the Prime Minister on Dec. 1, 1931, that complete provincial autonomy will be given to the provinces it is very necessary that our community should also keep pace with the times and so we should reconsider the decision which we arrived at before the statement of the Prime Minister referred to above.'

**

16. The Hindustan Times

Delhi

29-2-1932

Future of the Depressed Classes

The Working Committee of the All-India Depressed Classes Association, at a meeting held recently in Delhi, passed a number of important resolutions, in connection with the rights and demands of the community, in the new constitution. Most of the Committee's decisions are commendable, based as they are, on the sound principles of direct election, franchise on a population basis and joint electorates. But it is a matter of regret that the programme, outlined at the meeting, taken as a whole, lacks fire. To put it briefly, it is not at all a fighting programme. And it was a fighting programme that the All-India Depressed Classes Association should have devised, in consideration of the serious nature of the disruptive forces that have been released by Dr. Ambedkar and his following, however small or insignificant they might be. Dr. Ambedkar, as ill-luck would have it, has followed his own methods and convictions regardless of the major interests of those he claims to represent. Under these circumstances we cannot help feeling that the Working Committee has failed to avail itself of the present occasion to present a fighting programme to the community in its task of asserting its rights and privileges and making its influence felt.

The question of renaming the depressed classes as 'Adi-Hindus' in the new constitution, is really not of so much importance as the shaping of the future political and social destiny of the community. Dr. Ambedkar is tenaciously attempting to communalise the depressed classes for all practical purposes, for all time to come, thereby perpetuating the stigma of untouchability on its brow. The social stigma of the community has persisted long enough; but the political stigma which threatens to be the certain result of Dr. Ambedkar's handiwork, would be ruinous to the community's inherent and natural right to take its proper place in a free and self-governing India. Adult franchise is, of course, the only hope of the complete political uplift of the depressed classes. As a matter of fact, franchise on an adult population basis would benefit most the destitute or backward sections of the Indian population, who have been deprived so long of the usual qualifications for franchise. The indirect or group system of franchise cannot help them to liberate themselves from their political bondage to their overlords or those who are placed in the higher grades of the Indian social hierarchy. As regards the social or rather civic aspect of the demands of the depressed classes, any Declaration of Fundamental

Rights in the constitution, acceptable to the nation will be incomplete without a clear recognition of these rights. But before the depressed classes can achieve the excellent ideals set forth in the resolutions under consideration, they must be up and doing and bestir themselves. Mahatma Gandhi has pledged even to lay down his life to regenerate the community, not by a process of cutting it off from the rest of Hindu society as a separate political unit, but by a healthy and normal process of raising up its status. The whole nation is, therefore, committed to the uplift of the depressed classes, but the community itself must stand by the nation and refuse to be led by short-sighted political time-servers or by foolish hopes of any temporary communal gain.

**

17. The Hindustan Times

Delhi

29-2-1932

Depressed Classes for Joint Electorates

Moonje-Rajah Pact

Message sent to Premier & Lord Lothian

(From Our Special Correspondent)

Delhi, Saturday

I learn that the following cablegram has been dispatched jointly by Dr. B.S. Moonje, President, All-India Hindu Mahasabha and Mr. M.C. Rajah, President, All-India Depressed Classes Association, to the Prime Minister of England.

The same message has been repeated to Lord Lothian, Chairman of the Indian Franchise Committee.

The message reads:-

"Regarding the demand of separate electorates by Dr. Ambedkar, the Working Committee of the All-India Depressed Classes Association was held in Delhi on 21st and 22nd instant, and unanimously decided for joint electorates with Hindus, with reservation of seats on popular (population) basis.

"Complete agreement now prevails between the Depressed Classes Association and the Hindu Mahasabha. Letter follows."

New Delhi

C.T.O

25th February 1932.

Indian News Agency Telegram

No. 48(D)

New Delhi, dated 25th February 1932. Timed 20-25 hours.

New Delhi, 25th. In Consultative Committee Mr. Benthall raised question of discrimination between residents in various provinces as regards civic rights and exercise of trades or callings in provinces other than those in which they reside. After some discussion it was agreed that prohibition of such discrimination was desirable and that its details should be left to Parliamentary draftsman. Committee agreed that change of faith should not of itself render any person liable to loss of any civic right or entail any penalty. Committee further agreed to liberty of minorities to establish and control charitable, religious, social and educational institutions at their own expense, with right to exercise therein their religion and freely to use their own language. Committee accepted claim of depressed classes that any custom or usage whereby any disadvantage or disability is imposed upon, or any discrimination made against, any citizen in respect of enjoyment of civic rights, should be declared illegal.

Understood pact been signed between Mr. Moonje, representing All India Hindu Mahasabha and M.C. Rajah, representing All Indian Depressed Classes Association agreeing to representation of depressed classes through joint electorate with reservation of seats on population basis. This agreement is being cabled to premier under joint signature of both.

**

18. The Hindustan Times

Delhi

9-3-32

Rajah-Moonje Pact

Hindu and Sikh M.L.A.'s to Support

New Delhi, Sunday

At a meeting of Hindu and Sikh members of the Central Legislature and other Hindu leaders held at Dr. Moonje's residence, the pact recently made between Dr. Moonje and Rao Bahadur M.C. Rajah, regarding the representation of the Depressed Classes in legislatures through a joint electorate with reservation of seats on a population basis was approved, and it was decided to give Mr. Rajah and the Working Committee of the All-India Depressed Classes Association every support.

Protection of Minorities

Among those present at the meeting were Sir Hari Singh Gour, Rao Bahadur M.C. Rajah, Diwan Bahadur Harbilas Sarda, Dr. Radhakumud Mukerjee, Mr. Amarnath Dutt, Mr. D.K. Lahiri Choudhry, Prof. Chablani, Rajah Sir Rampal Singh, Lala Sri Ram, Lala Jagannath Agarwal, Lala Narayan Dutt, Sardar Sant Singh, M. Gupteswar Prasad, Mr. Gaya Prasad Singh, Lala Harivansh, Mr. B.N. Misra and Mr Ganpat Rai.

After the approval of the Pact, Dr. Radhakumud Mukerjee addressed the meeting, which adopted the following further resolutions:-

(1) that all minority problems should be solved preferably on a basis of minorities guarantee treaties of the League of Nations to which both England and India are already parties as members of the League;

(2) that this meeting is fundamentally opposed to separate electorates for any community;

(3) that there ought to be no reservation of seats either in joint or separate electorates for any community, which is in a majority in any province;

(4) that in any scheme for protection of minorities by reservation of seats, the representation of any minority community in any province in the provincial legislature, should under no circumstances be fixed below its proportion to the population of the province; and

(5) That in any scheme of weightage for minorities, it should be fixed on the principle, equally applicable to all minorities.

It is understood, that Mr. M.C. Rajah and Dr. Moonje have sent a joint letter to the Prime Minister, confirming the cable regarding the Pact.

Rajah-Moonje Pact

Delhi, Monday

It is understood that Dr. B.S. Moonje has sent a letter to Mr. Ramsay MacDonald, confirming his cable with regard to the agreement arrived at between Dr. Moonje and Rao Bahadur M.C. Rajah.

**

19. The Tribune
Lahore
10-3-1932

Notes and Comments

The Moonje-Rajah Pact

It is gratifying to find that a meeting of Hindu and Sikh members of the Central Legislature and other Hindu leaders recently held at Delhi approved of the pact made between Dr. Moonje and Mr. Rajah regarding the representation of the depressed classes in the Legislature through joint electorates with a reservation of seats on a population basis, and decided to give Mr. Rajah and the Working Committee of the All-India Depressed Classes Association every support. Joint electorates with a reservation of seats is admittedly a half-way house between the present arrangement and the complete elimination of communal representation, but it has this great advantage over separate electorates that unlike the latter, which is calculated to perpetuate communal representation, it can pave the way to the complete disappearance of that vicious principle.

**

20. The Indian Daily Mail

Bombay

9-3-1932

Communalists Hit

The Moonje-Rajah Pact has been further strengthened by its being ratified by the Sikh and Hindu leaders who are anxious to weld the whole Hindu community into one. At a meeting in Delhi many of the orthodox pillars of the Hindu community as well as of the Sikh put their signatures to the Pact and thus supported the case of the Congress for joint electorates. This ought to cut off the ground from under the feet of communalists, to whatever class or community they may belong, as also of the reactionaries in England and India who are beckoning them to their help. We do not know what Dr. Ambedkar will now do with his newly formed alliance with Mr. S. Ali and members of the ruling community. Dr. Moonje has cabled to the Premier of this Pact, though it is not likely to have any healthy effect on the Premier and affect greatly his decision on the communal question which has been so foolishly left to his arbitration, as he, more than anybody else, has been mainly responsible for the fictitious importance it has acquired.

The Pact ought to remove many misunderstandings, and make the whole position clear. With the elimination of the Adi-Hindus there is only one group of any importance in the field now and that is the Muslim communalist group, whose influence in India is diminishing daily, as Muslims are realising more and more that the future of the country is inseparably bound with joint electorates. Dr. Ambedker wants to give statutory sanction to the "Depressed Classes" so that he can raise himself to eminence on their humiliations. To relegate these classes permanently to the backwaters of Hinduism, would not only be a blunder but a gross crime which every Indian, to whatever community he may belong, ought not to countenance for a moment.

The Delhi meeting passed a number of resolutions of fundamental importance, which ought to form the basis of any constitution which is intended to have a lasting influence on the country. The meeting was opposed to separate electorates for any community in India, and this reaffirmation of the Congress decision ought to go a long way in defeating the object of the separatists. The minority problems are to be solved on the basis of "Minorities Guarantee treaties to which both England and India are already parties as members of the League of Nations. There is influential opinion in the country which wanted the issue of minority representation, if not solved by the communities themselves, to be referred to the League of Nations or the Hague Tribunal for their decision. That would have effectively taken the matter out of the hands of interested parties like the present Prime Minister.

**

21. The Madras Mail

Madras

7-3-1932

The Lost Leader

After communing with his inner mentor, Mr. M.C. Rajah not long ago achieved a startling volte face. He who had been the champion of separate electorates as the only reliable means of protecting the Depressed Classes against the dominance of the majority community, announced that he was converted to the necessity for joint electorates with reservation of seats. Three weeks after the publication of this highly interesting revelation, Mr. Rajah concluded a pact with Dr. Moonje, the leader of the Mahasabhites, and joined with that astute gentleman in sending a cable to England to the Prime Minister, announcing the terms of the agreement. Now Mr. Rajah has obtained the benediction of Hindu and Sikh members of the Central Legislature and of other Hindu leaders. Perhaps he is content. But we would seriously suggest to Mr. Rajah that he should have first secured the approval of those whom he seeks to represent before he sought the alliance of those whose approval was a foregone conclusion. If Mr. Rajah had achieved some striking compromise he might then approach his nominal constituents with some sense of satisfaction and in the legitimate hope of securing conversions as the result of his endeavours on their behalf.

But he seems to have made no attempt to secure support from the Depressed Classes beforehand. In a communication, published elsewhere, from the Secretary of the Depressed Classes Society, New Delhi, it is stated that, in the very meeting from which Mr. Rajah secured his mandate to conclude the pact with Dr. Moonje, and which cannot be called completely representative by any stretch of imagination, there was difference of opinion.

The objections of the Adi-Hindus to joint electorates are well known. They fear that even reservation of seats will not free them from domination by the caste majority. They want representatives who are responsible to, and can be called to account by themselves and not by a large constituency in which they, owing to disabilities occasioned by illiteracy and other handicaps to the exercise of the vote, will form a relatively small and uninfluential majority. The example of Mr. Rajah himself will give pause to any notions which they may entertain of the consistency of representatives for whose election they have not been directly responsible. Consciously or unconsciously, such representatives will, though members of a minority community themselves, voice the views of the majority.

In the resolutions adopted at the benedictory meeting in New Delhi this weekend, there is one calling attention to the Minorities guarantee treaties of the League of Nations. This gives a fine air of impartiality to the proceedings. But it is worthy of a closer examination to discover what these treaties do, in fact, guarantee. The first, and more generally applicable type of these guarantees safeguards the right to nationality and to life, personal liberty and freedom of worship, equality before the law and in civil and political rights, rights to the use of a minority language, opportunity to enter public employment, and appropriate provisions for education in the language of the minority. There are other special rights for specially situated communities. It will be seen, however, that none of these enumerated includes the special problem of electorates. Very proper and necessary as provisions of this kind may be, they are better fitted for inclusion in some such Fundamental Rules as those recently discussed by the Consultative Committee of the Round Table Conference. But it is some more special form of political protection, specially adapted to ensure that they shall exercise adequate influence in the Legislatures, which the Adi-Hindus seek. The vast majority of the politically conscious among them have decided that such protection may be obtained from separate electorates. Mr. Rajah's own personal conviction is valueless without his community's endorsement.

**

22. The Madras Mail
Madras
7-3- 1932

"REPUDIATED" PACT

The Depressed Classes

Moonje-Rajah Agreement "Not Binding"

Mr. M.S. Chotti Ram, Secretary of the Depressed Classes Society, New Delhi, writes as follows:

The Working Committee of the All-India Depressed Classes Association met at Delhi recently under the president-ship of Mr. M.C. Rajah, and the meeting was attended mainly by petty leaders. Mr. Gavai was also present. Assam and Bengal were not represented in the Committee, while Bombay and Madras, where caste oppression is very great, were not represented by any one of their leaders in the Legislatures or by a known leader. It seemed as if Mr. Rajah and his few lieutenants were the only representatives of the whole of India, and this meeting was evidently got up by them.

Mr. Rajah stated to a Press representative that in that meeting the consensus of opinion was in favour of joint electorates. This was not correct. There was a difference of opinion among the members, and as nothing could be decided at that meeting, it was agreed to call a special conference of the Depressed Classes at Nagpur to discuss the matter at length.

Give and Take Policy

A resolution was also passed that "the Committee do not agree with the Minority Pact with reference to the number of seats fixed for Bengal, the Central Provinces, the Punjab, and the United Provinces". When the representatives of the Depressed Classes at the Round Table Conference allocated the number of seats, they took an impartial course by distributing the seats according to the degree of caste oppression in the Provinces and the distribution of population. Further, they had to follow a policy of give and take with other Minorities when they entered into an agreement and signed the Minority Pact. If at all any partiality was shown to any particular Province, that could be easily adjusted if the matter is brought in the proper way to the notice of the Depressed Classes delegate to the Conference. In any case, this on no account could serve as a reason for disagreement with so important a pact as the Minority Pact.

Mr. Rajah has evidently played into the hands of Dr. Moonje and the Hindu Mahasabha. Since the All India Depressed Classes Association has no office-bearers elected by the Depressed Classes of India, and has no branches in the Provinces, the pact of its self-elected leader (Mr. M.C. Rajah) with Dr. Moonje is not binding upon the Depressed Classes. The Pact was concluded by two individuals whose leadership is repudiated in Madras, Bengal and several other Provinces, without either the consent or consultation of Dr. Ambedkar and Rao Bahadur Srinivasan, the real representatives of the Depressed Classes. The Depressed Classes and the Government will therefore do well to ignore this so-called Pact. Mr. Rajah's changed attitude at this juncture is to be condemned. Whether he will perform another somersault is yet to be seem.

Separate Electorate

Claims of Depressed Classes in Bengal

A resolution urging separate electorates for the Depressed Classes was passed at the annual conference of that community in Bengal held recently in Calcutta. Mr. Mukunda Beharry Mullick, M.L.C., presided.

The conference was against reservation of seats in a joint electorate for the backward classes for, it was maintained, in such a case there would "hardly be any chance of a true representative of the depressed classes being elected to the legislatures."

"The attempt on the part of a few caste Hindus to create division among the depressed classes," was condemned by the meeting.

The conference repudiated the claim of Rao Bahadur M.C. Rajah to speak on behalf of the depressed classes in support of joint electorates.

"Not Representative"

The "All-India" Association

Mr. M.B. Mullick, M.L.C., (President, Bengal Depressed Classes Association), Mr. Nanak Chand Dhusa (President U.P. Adi-Hindu (Depressed Classes) Association, Mr. Sonadhar Das Senapati, (President, All-Assam Depressed Classes Association), Mr. Hari Ram, (Vice-President Adi-Dharam Depressed Classes Mandal, Punjab), and Mr. Sultan Ram, (President Bihar and Orissa Depressed Classes Association), have sent the following letter to the Press regarding the All-India Depressed Classes Association:

'It is reported that a meeting of the Working Committee of the All-India Depressed Classes' Association was held on February 21 in New Delhi at which Mr. Rajah explained his grounds for supporting joint electorates for the Depressed Classes and that at that meeting the consensus of opinion was in favour of joint electorates.

"We wish to take this opportunity to state that the so-called All-India Depressed Classes' Association is not representative of the Depressed

Classes of India. It has no Branches in the Provinces except in the C.P., Bombay and Madras and even in these Provinces there are no members except the office-bearers. We do not know how representative this gathering was and whether the Depressed Classes from the Provinces were present. We know that those from Assam and Bengal did not attend the meeting. Mr. Rajah was the staunchest supporter of separate electorates as late as November last and we do not know what has led him to change his views.

"Regarding the statement of Mr. Rajah that there was a consensus of opinion in favour of joint electorates, we wish to state that this is not the case and that we representing the Depressed Classes of the Provinces of Assam, Bengal, U.P., Behar and Orissa and Punjab still stand for and insist upon separate electorate for the Depressed Classes."

**

23. The Hindustan Times
Delhi
18-3-1932

"Long Live Moonje-Rajah Pact"
Depressed Classes' Procession in Bombay

Bombay, March 16.

A procession led by Mr. Deorukhker, a nationalist Depressed Class leader, belonging to the joint electorate school, started from Matunga at about 11:30 a.m. and after parading through the important thoroughfares on cycles, lorries, cars, etc. and carrying posters, reached the Town Hall by about 2 p.m. Along the route, the processionists shouted "Long Live Moonje-Rajah Pact and Joint Electorate." They also shouted "Boycott Ambedkar and Solanki."

On arrival at the Town Hall Mr. Deorukhker interviewed the Lothian Committee which was in session. The procession then dispersed peacefully. The procession was taken to demonstrate the Depressed Classes' overwhelming sympathy for joint electorates.

Two of the demonstrators it is reported were arrested — Free Press.

**

24. The Hindustan Times

Delhi

19-3-1932

The Moonje-Rajah Pact

Critics Answered

Rai Bahadur M.C. Rajah's Statement

New Delhi, Thursday.

Reminding his critics how another Nair-Rajah Pact succeeded in the interest of the Depressed Classes, Rao Bahadur M.C. Rajah answers, in a statement to the Press, critics of the Moonje-Rajah Pact.

He expresses satisfaction at the reception given by his community to the Pact with Dr. Moonje, and answers his detractors.

"I will not follow", he says "the line adopted by my critics by imputing to them personal motives. For me, it is enough to state facts that must tell their tale."

"In 1917 in the wake of the Great War, the late Dr. Nair, leader of the non-Brahmin movement in Madras, wishing to rally the Depressed Classes to the banner of the Justice Party in view of the then imminent constitutional changes, extended his hand of fellowship to me, and desired that the Depressed Classes of the Madras Presidency should join his movement.

"I was then the Secretary of the Madras Adi-Dravida Mahajan Sabha, with Mr. P.V. Subrammayam Pillai as its President.

A Political Pact

"I entered into a compact with Mr. Nair that was a political pact, unwritten, like most popular compacts, between the Adi-Dravidas and the non-Brahmin caste Hindus, a compact effected for mutual benefit.

"Then there were some amongst us who asked themselves whether it was wise to join the non-Brahmins, seeing that they were our oppressors. They howled and hooted at me and accused me of bartering my community to the heartless non-Brahmins. They started rival organizations to mine, such as the Dravida Mahajan Sabha, wrote petitions against me to the Governor of Madras and against my Association. They accused me and vilified me.

Justice Party's Help

"When Dr. Nair gave the necessary awakening and the necessary call to the Depressed Classes, the Justice Party did help my community. When their representative, Sir K.V. Reddy and Diwan Bahadur Ramaswami

Mudaliar, appeared before the Joint Parliamentary Committee, they had the kindness to place our case before that Committee in London. When the Justice Party came into power, they did not neglect our interests, though they could have done more for us.

"Seeing the good offices of the Justice Party towards the Depressed Classes, the very gentleman who accused me of my compact with Dr. Nair and who worked against the Justice Party candidates in the Legislative Council elections then, gradually came into the Justice Party and today they hail the Justice Party as the champion of the Depressed Classes.

History Will Repeat Itself

"I have no hesitation is saying that history will repeat itself. Those that abuse me now and carry on a mischievous propaganda will soon realize the importance and usefulness of the Pact I have made with the Hindu Mahasabha, and will follow the footsteps of my Madras brethren who are now enjoying the beneficence of the Justice Party.

"I was not blind to the fact when I made this Pact that there would be some opposition from certain sections of the Depressed Classes, for the obvious reason that only a very few of my community are fully aware of the present day politics, and the quick succession of changing circumstances. How many persons belonging to the Depressed Classes are in possession of what took place at the Round Table Conference and what takes place in several committees that are now working in India.

Serving his community

"Taking stock of all the facts, I could not but take this step in the best interests of my community. I need not say that I have been all the year working for the welfare of the community to the best of my ability."

"To take the opportunity by the forelock is a golden rule for success. Unless we risk, no profit can be gained. Suspicion breeds suspicion. Every one of us has to live in our mother country. My humble suggestion is that at this juncture, to advise the community to mark the time for political advance when others are going forward with rapid strides, will be putting a brake in the progress of the community itself.

"Let us all put our shoulders together to bring the community almost in line with the other communities of India"— A.P.I.

**

25. The Times of India

Bombay

15-3-1932

The Munje-Rajah Pact
Splitting Depressed Classes

To the Editor of "The Time of India"

Sir,— Though Dr. Munje and the Hindu Maha Sabha have been unable to wipe out the blot of untouchability from Hinduism and thus to make the Hindu organisation strong and compact, they have succeeded in trapping a leader of the Depressed Classes with a view to causing a split in the ranks of those classes. The Munje-Rajah pact is being boosted by the Congress and Maha-Sabha organs, and it is being represented to the gullible public that the pact is being supported by the majority of the depressed class people. In fact, the Munje-Rajah pact is being strongly denounced by almost all the accredited leaders and leading organisations of the depressed classes in the country. The Congress and Maha- Sabha organs have, however, made a conspiracy to suppress all news about the vehement opposition the pact is evoking.

It was Rao Bahadur M.C. Rajah who was strongly in favour of separate electorate when Dr. Ambedkar was advocating joint electorates and reserved seats, and it was through pressure from Mr. Rajah and the depressed class organisations in the Madras Presidency, that Dr. Ambedkar had to set his personal views aside and to make a demand for separate representation at the Round Table Conference. He received support in his demand from Mr. Rajah who in a speech only some weeks back gave his opinion that the salvation of the depressed classes lay only in separate electorates. His latest somersault was a surprise to all. He entered into a pact for joint electorates and reserved seats with the leader of the Hindu Maha Sabha without consulting the other leaders and the responsible organisation of the depressed classes in the different provinces. Nor has he given any reasons justifying his new policy. The fact that Dr. Ambedkar was greeted with a rousing reception and was supported in his demand for separate representation by thousands of people recently at Madras itself, is sufficient to prove that Rao Bahadur Rajah lacks support even in his own presidency. The evidence which is being given before the Franchise Committee also proves beyond dispute that an overwhelming majority of the depressed classes is in favour of separate electorates.

The Bombay Congress and Maha Sabha organs have given out that Mr. B.J. Deorukhkar has sent a memorandum to the Franchise Committee signed by over five thousand people belonging to the depressed classes in support of the Munje-Rajah pact. It has, however, been discovered this is nothing but fiction. The fact is that a few set replies to the questionnaire issued by the Franchise Committee have been forwarded in the name of certain insignificant bodies, the numerical strength of which is quite negligible. Mr. Deorukhkar represents himself and at the most some people belonging to his sub-section of the Chamar community, viz., the Dabholi Chamars who constitute but a small fraction of the so-called untouchable community in Maharashtra.

We challenge the Congress and Maha Sabha people and their friends in the depressed classes to prove their majority in a public meeting specially held for the purpose. So long as they are not prepared to do this the claims of the Congress and Maha Sabha organs should be treated with the contempt they deserve.

Divakar Pagare (Mahar),

K.G. Chandorker (Chambhar)

**

26. The Hindustan Times

Delhi

17-3-32

Moonje-Rajah Pact

Depressed Classes Support

Delhi, Tuesday

On behalf of the Shradhanand Memorial Trust, a conference of the depressed classes was held at Bagichi Raghunath, at which resolutions were passed, supporting the Moonje-Rajah Pact.

**

27. The Indian Daily Mail
Bombay
18-3-1932

"Down With Dr. Ambedkar"
Depressed Classes' Demonstration

Bombay, Wednesday

"Long Live Rajah-Moonje Pact."

"Down with Dr. Ambedkar."

"Down with Dr. Solanki."

"We don't Want Separate Electorates."

Placards bearing the above inscriptions, displayed in motor-lorries, were seen moving this noon in the Fort area. More than eight lorries carried members of the depressed classes, who kept on shouting slogans condemning the alleged tactics of Dr. Ambedkar.

About fifty cyclists formed the vanguard of the procession. Even women were heard shouting slogans from the moving motor-lorries. This created quite a sensation in the Fort area.

When they reached the Town Hall, a number of policemen armed with lathis led by a few sergeants confronted them and prevented their progress. Fearing a lathi charge, the men began to run, when Mr. B.J. Deorurkar, who was leading the procession had a parley with the police officers. The procession was reformed and returned to Mazagaon after demonstrating all along the route.

**

28. The Hindustan Times

Delhi

23-3-32

More Support For Mr. Rajah

Dr. Ambedkar's Claims Repudiated

(From Our Correspondent).

Patna, March 20.

At a public meeting of the Gowalia Mochis of Patna, under the presidentship of Gopi Bhagat, of Manshram ka Akhara, in Patna city, resolutions were passed condemning the proposal of a separate electorate for the depressed classes, repudiating the claims of Dr. Ambedkar to the leadership of the depressed classes, and expressing confidence is the leadership of Rao Bahadur M.C. Rajah, M.L.A., President of the All India Depressed Classes Association.

**

29. The Leader
Allahabad
23-3-32

Depressed Classes
Feeling in Favour of Joint Electorate
Impression on Lothian Committee
Significant District Boards' Election Results in Madras

(From Our Correspondent)

New Delhi, March 21.

According to reports received here Lord Lothian and his colleagues have been struck by the strength of the feeling amongst the depressed classes which backs the Rajah-Moonje Pact. I am told that the Bombay anti-Ambedkar demonstrations have particularly been an eye-opener to the committee. Another factor of importance in this connection has just occurred in the first election under the Madras District Boards Act which has given the depressed classes joint electorate with reservation of seats. These show, for instance, in the Chingleput district of the Madras presidency, that the Depressed Classes association nominees have both captured two seats reserved for the depressed classes and that they are hopeful of capturing even one or two un-reserved seats. The successful candidates include Rao Bahadur M.C. Rajah himself, who being president of the All-India Depressed Classes Association and the originator of joint electorates schemes naturally feels that this endorsement by his constituency of his programme as against Dr. Ambedkar is not without its significance.

**

30. The Hindustan Times

Delhi

24-3-932

Moonje-Rajah Pact

Hindu Sabha's Appreciation

Akola, March 22.

The Provincial Hindu Sabha Working Committee, Berar, met at Akola on Sunday, the 20th March and expressed its deep appreciation at the services rendered by Doctor Moonje in entering into a pact with R.B. M.C. Rajah, the Nationalist leader of the Depressed Classes and making him agree to the Joint Electorates.

**

31. The Hindustan Times

Delhi

25-3-1932

Depressed Classes Want Joint Electorates

Mr. M.C. Rajah's Letter to the Premier

New Delhi, Wednesday

In a letter to Prime Minister, Mr. Ramsay MacDonald, Rao Bahadur M.C. Rajah declares that even his proposal for joint electorate with reservation of seats is a temporary expedient till his community which is an integral part of Hindu society is able to stand on its legs.

The letter of Mr. Rajah runs:-

"I have great pleasure in confirming the wire sent jointly by myself as President of the Depressed classes Association and Dr. B.S. Moonje, President of the All-India Hindu Mahasabha. The wire is as follows:-

"Regarding demand separate electorates by Dr. Ambedkar Working Committee of All-India Depressed classes Association was held Delhi 21st and 22nd and unanimously decided for joint electorates with Hindus with reservation seats on population basis. Complete agreement now prevails between Depressed classes Association, and Hindu Mahasabha Letter follows."

"The All-India Depressed classes Association is the only central organisation of the Depressed classes established in 1925. Ever since the association has been holding annual sessions at various centres in India laying down the policy on behalf of the Depressed classes for the whole of India. I am its President and I have had the honour of presiding over its conferences in 1925, 1928 and 1931. I was invited to serve on the Committee of the Indian Legislature known as the Indian Central Committee to cooperate with the Indian Statutory Commission in 1928. I was a member of the Madras Legislative Council from 1919 till 1926 and from 1927 I have been a member of the Indian Legislative Assembly, representing the Depressed Classes.

"The Hindu Mahasabha is the organised body of the Hindus, taken as a whole, representing them in matters like removal of untouchability and social and religious relations of the Hindus with the Depressed classes of the community Dr. B.S. Moonje is the President of the Mahasabha. He was a member of the Central Provinces Legislative Council from 1923 to 1926. In 1926 he became a member of the Indian Legislative Assembly which position he held (...cannot be read). He is a member of the Round Table Conference. He had the honour of presiding over the Conferenee of the Hindu Mahasabha in 1926; and since then he has been elected its Working President every year.

"I pointed out in my note appended to the Report of the Indian Central Committee in September 1929 that the peaceful progress of the Untouchable classes is a *sine qua non* of the orderly development of Indian nationalism and that paradoxical as it may sound, the aim of the Depressed classes and those working for their uplift is the abolition of their distinction so that they should become one with the Hindu society — an indistinguishable part of that body. Individual social reformers were ploughing their lonely furrows and it was only when a growing interest was taken by the people in the politics of the country that the desire for reforms became general and insistent. A most hopeful sign is the practical unanimity with which educated Hindu India has now come to condemn the social subservice (*sic*) of those people.

Fighting Untouchability

Now the Hindu Mahasabha, for the first time in the social and constitutional history of India, officially invited the All-India Depressed Classes Association to join them to work on a common platform and to do away with the curse of untouchability. This I cannot but consider as an earnest attempt on the part of the caste Hindus to remove the bane of untouchability from among the Hindus.

As this juncture to refuse the hand of fraternity extended to the depressed classes by our co-religionists, the caste Hindus will not be conductive to a healthy growth of my community whose evolution to a footing of equality is the be all and end all of our ambitions and activities. The invitation of the Hindu Mahasabha is a happy sign, and it is in consonance with the resolutions passed in their Conference in Jubbulpore in April1928, which clearly shows an indication of an awakening of the Hindu social conscience.

In the circumstances I find that a ray of hope of our assimilation into the main body of the Hindus is appearing in the political horizon of the country and I fervently hope and trust that the realisation of this ideal is not very distant. To stand in the way of realisation of this, our cherished goal will not only be impolitic but also suicidal on our part.

Moreover, I feel that other minority communities desire to strengthen their separate interests by taking advantage of the backward condition of the depressed classes and persuading them to adopt a course which will lead to permanent division and prevent the growth of any feeling of political as well as social oneness and solidarity amongst the Hindus.

Forces of Democracy

As the forces of democracy in India are proceeding with rapid strides and as ere long full provincial autonomy will be in full swing every community in the country has to adjust itself to the rapid changing circumstances. The desire for separate electorates for the depressed classes was made at a time when it was expected that there would still be tutelary period with the reserve side of the Government and that the Government would continue as the special protector of the minority interests as heretofore. If the entire Government in the provinces is to be made responsible to the legislature a small minority, like the Depressed Classes should it cling to its separateness, will have to be permanently in the opposition. In the case of Muslims the fact that they constitute an effective percentage makes it impossible for them to be ignored altogether, whereas a combination between the caste Hindus and the Muslims will for ever prevent any minority like ours from being able to get any share of the political power. This fear is strengthened by the fact that in daily life the Muslims treat the untouchables as badly as Hindus.

Besides the representatives of the minority communities will have opportunities for service only when they merge themselves in a common electorate and subscribe to a common political view.

An Understanding

The two associations, that is, the All-India Depressed Classes' Association on the one side and the All-India Hindu Mahasabha on the other, having come to an understanding among ourselves on the basis of joint electorates with reserved seats according to their proportion of population, there ought to be no question now of granting separate electorates for the depressed classes. The depressed classes have to come to know that under the so-called Minorities Pact that was made in London, they cannot get their full share of seats in the legislatures in proportion to their number in the population; while under the system of joint electorates, they not only get their full reservation but obtain also the right of contesting additional seats and also of powerfully influencing the entire Hindu elections, thereby giving an additional impetus to the removal of untouchability.

An analysis of the figures in the annexure contained in the Minority Pact referred to above, relating to seats earmarked in the various provinces for the Depressed Classes, shows that Dr. Ambedkar and Rao Bahadur Srinivasan have taken weightage for themselves and ignored the rights of the depressed classes in the provinces of Punjab, Bengal, Central Provinces and United Province and also where the depressed classes are allotted seats less than their proportion in the population. This arrangement with the Hindu Mahasabha rectifies this discrimination and does equal justice to the depressed classes all over India.

Temporary Expedient

I take this opportunity to make it clear that even this proposal of reservation of seats is merely of the nature of a temporary expedient. I hope and believe that, in view of the present awakening in my community, they will soon realise their inherent strength and will be able to stand on their legs, rubbing shoulders in healthy competition with other sections of the Hindu society, of which we are, as I have said above, quite an integral part.

In this connection I may mentioned that, when the late Mr. Montague came out to India, the demand of the non-Brahmins of the Madras Presidency was for separate electorates, but they were given reservation of seats in joint electorates. Today, however, they do not stand in need of this protection. I have no doubt a similar experiment in our case also will lead to healthy development.

I have, therefore, to request you to note the fact that the depressed classes do not demand separate electorates, but want joint electorates with the Hindus and reservation of seats on the population basis—A.P.I

**

32. The Tribune

Lahore

25-3-1932

"The Best Solution"

The one solid achievement of the forces of reaction and retrogression at the second Round Table Conference was the so-called Minorities Pact, and the most noticeable thing about that pact, that which gave all its importance to it, was the association with it of Dr. Ambedkar, who claimed to represent the depressed classes. Mr. M.C. Rajah's letter to the Prime Minister, confirming the cable sent by him jointly with Dr. Moonje, finally pricks this Ambedkar bubble, and with it sounds the death-knell of the Minorities Pact itself, so far, at any rate, as the depressed classes are concerned. Mr. Rajah points out that the All-India Depressed Classes Association, on behalf of which he has now entered into a pact with Dr. Moonje as representing the All India Hindu Mahasabha, is the only central organisation of to the depressed classes, that he is its President and has thrice presided over its annual Conferences, that since 1927 he has been a member of the Indian Legislative Assembly representing the depressed classes, and that in that capacity he was invited to serve on the Indian Central Committee, an adjunct of the Statutory Commission, in 1928. Obviously the claim of Dr. Ambedkar to speak for the depressed classes cannot for a moment be pitted against that of Mr. M.C., Rajah and the Association of which he is the President. When such a man declares in the most unequivocal terms that he and his Association are against separate electorates, the basic principle of the Minorities Pact, the Prime Minister is bound to take that declaration as the final verdict of the depressed classes.

But Mr. Rajah does not rest his case merely on his unchallengeable credentials. He also supports it by arguments of a conclusive character. In the forefront of these he places the undeniable fact that the course which the other minorities had, in order to strengthen their own separate interests, persuaded the depressed classes delegates to adopt, "would lead to a permanent division and prevent the growth of any feeling of political as well as social oneness and solidarity amongst the Hindus." This, as every one knows, was the most important ground on which Mahatma Gandhi stoutly resisted the Pact at the Round Table Conference. "The claims advanced on behalf of the untouchables," he said, "mean a perpetual bar-sinister. I would not sell the vital interests of the untouchables even for the sake of winning the freedom of India." Again: — "We do not want on our registers and on our census untouchables classified as a separate class. Sikhs may remains as such in perpetuity, so may Muslims, so may Europeans. Will untouchables remain untouchables in perpetuity? I would far rather that Hinduism died than that untouchability lived." This impassioned plea failed to make any impression on Dr. Ambedkar, who had made up his mind that the vital, permanent interests of his community must be sacrificed for the temporary advantage of a part of it; and so did Mahatma Gandhi's assertion that if there was a referendum he would not only get the vote of the untouchables but would top the poll. The Mahatma was given no opportunity, on his return to India, to make good his claim, but Mr. Rajah and the All-India Depressed Classes Association have shown conclusively by the action they have taken that the Mahatma's claim was abundantly justified.

Of course, in the decision which Mr. Rajah and the Depressed Classes Association have reached the changed attitude of the caste Hindus themselves has had no inconsiderable share. As Mr. Rajah points out, the Hindus Mahasabha, which represents the caste Hindus as no other organisation in India does, has, for the first time in the social and constitutional history of India, invited the All India Depressed Classes Association to join them to work on a common platform and to do away with the curse of untouchability. Mr. Rajah is perfectly justified in considering this action on the part of the Hindu Mahasabha as an earnest attempt on the part of the caste Hindus to remove the ban of untouchability in Hindu society. To refuse the hand of fellowship thus extended to the depressed classes by the caste Hindus would obviously be detrimental not only to the interests of the Hindu community and with it of the country as a whole, but to the healthy growth of the depressed classes themselves, whose elevation to a footing of equality with the so-called higher castes is "the be-all and end-all of all their ambitions and activities." And what, after all, do the depressed classes lose by being thus assimilated in the general Hindu community? Mr. Rajah has no difficulty in showing that so far from losing anything they gain all along the line. The so-called Minorities Pact did not give them even their full population share of seats. The reason why Dr. Ambedkar and Mr. Srinivasan agreed to it was, as we now know, the promise of weightage given to them in their own Province. This weightage as Mr. Rajah shows, was purchased at the expense of their brethren elsewhere. The scheme which Mr. Rajah and Dr. Moonje have agreed upon rectifies this discrimination and gives the depressed classes everywhere the proportion of seats to which they are entitled, though, of course, in joint electorates, besides giving them the right to contest as many additional seats as they like.

It requires no extraordinary perspicacity to see that even from the narrow point of view of their immediate political interests, to say nothing about their ultimate political and social well-being, this arrangement is much better than the one to which Dr. Ambedkar made himself a party. Mr. Rajah is, in our opinion, perfectly justified, in saying that considering all things this is the best solution for immediate, though not, of course, for ultimate purposes. So far as the latter are concerned, Mr. Rajah is under no delusion whatever. "I take this opportunity to make it clear," he says, "that even this proposal for a reservation of seats is merely in the nature of a temporary expedient. I hope and believe that in view of the present awakening in my community, they will soon realise their inherent strength and will be able to stand on their legs, rubbing shoulders in healthy competition with other sections of Hindu society, of which we are quite an integral part." If only the other minorities in India had the same wisdom, clear-headedness and sagacity that Mr. Rajah and his Association possess they would have come to exactly the same conclusion to which the latter have come. If the depressed classes are socially an integral part of the Hindu community, the Muslims and other non-Hindu Minorities are politically an equally integral part of the Indian nation; and every single argument that Mr. Rajah advances in favour of joint electorates with a reservation of seats as a temporary expedient holds as true in their case as in the case of the depressed classes.

**

33. The Statesman

Delhi

30-3-1932

New Delhi Procession

The All-India Shradhanand Dalit-uddhar Sabha yesterday took out a procession of 60 persons in New Delhi to demonstrate in favour of joint electorates for the depressed classes. New Delhi railway station was the starting point and the destination was the office of the Lothian Committee, where the processionists shouted *Bharat Mata-ki-jai* and *Hindu Dharam-ki-jai*.

The procession was watched by Lord Lothian and many spectators. The processionists carried flags on which were written in English, "We are Hindus of Hindus," "Separate Electorates Would be Suicidal to Our Social Uplift, Political Education and Progress;" "Welcome Moonje-Rajah Pact."

**

34. The Eastern Times

Lahore

30-3-32

The Minority Position

Never in the political history of this country has it been so important for the minority communities to present a united front against the aggression of the majority community as it is to-day, when the Congress is openly and unabashedly claiming to represent more than 80 per cent of the peoples of India, and by sheer dint of vociferation is in a fair way to get this preposterous claim accepted. It is for this reason that we consider the alliance between the All-India Depressed Classes Association and the Hindu Mahasabha, projected by the Depressed Class leader Rao Bahadur M.C. Rajah, as a major issue.

At the Round Table Conference, the depressed classes representative, Dr. Ambedkar, rightly took the view that the interests of the depressed classes were co-incident with those of the other minority communities, and acting on this well-founded belief he became, on behalf of his community, a party to the Minorities Pact, but since then powerful influences have been brought to bear on the other depressed class leaders, who come to believe that their interests are, not those of the other minorities, but of the Hindus. The arguments on which Mr. Rajah bases his view that the interest of the depressed classes lie in an alliance with the Hindus are specious and will not bear close examination.

"If the entire Government in the provinces is to be made responsible to the legislature," he says, " a small minority like the depressed classes, should it cling to a 'separate' policy, will have to be permanently in opposition. In the case of the Muslims, the fact that they constitute an effective percentage makes it impossible for them to be ignored altogether, whereas a combination between the caste Hindus and the Muslims will for ever prevent any minority like ours from being able to get any share of the political power." This argument might hold water were the hypothesis on which it is based even remotely true; but nowhere except in the imagination of Dr. Moonje and his dupes does the possibility exist that the Muslims, the guardians of the rights of the smaller minorities, would enter in to an alliance against them with the majority.

If Mr. Rajah and his depressed class friends really believe that "under the system of joint electorates, they would not only get their full reservation but would also obtain the right of contesting additional seats and powerfully influencing the entire Hindu election and thereby giving an additional impetus to the removal of untouchability," then they are more credulous than the ordinary run of men.

If under the old system, where the power for mischief of the Hindus was limited, they oppressed the depressed classes and denied them not only political but human rights there seems to be no reason why under the new constitution the majority community will be more considerate of those rights. No, the truth, which ought to be self evident is that the only efficient safeguard of minority rights lies in the alliance of the minorities against aggression by the majority community, and in adequate representation on a communal basis. But, of course this alliance need continue for such time only till the majority community proves by deeds and not by words or propaganda that it respects the rights and interest of minorities in the same manner as it does it own.

**

35. The Bombay Chronicle

Bombay

30-3-1932

More Support to Rajah-Moonje Pact

Representative Bombay Association's Wire To Lothian & Rajah Disowning Ambedkar's Lead.

The following wires have been sent to Lord Lothian and Rao Bahadur Rajah from Bombay:-

(1) From Mr. J.S. Kaj, the well known leader of Mayawanshi Samaj to Rao Bahadur Rajah, "Mayawanshi Samaj, Guzerati-speaking section, whole heartedly support Rajah-Munje Pact.

(2) From Mr. J.S. Kaj, to Lord Lothian, "We support Rajah Munje Pact."

(3) From M.D. Verman, President Rajput Sangathan Maha Sabha to Lord Lothian, "We support Rajah-Munje Pact". "No confidence in Ambedkar."

(4) From, Lakhala Waghela, Secretary, Bala Mitra Mandal, Walpakhadi, to Lord Lothian, Delhi. "Depressed classes want joint Electorates Adult Franchise and support Rajah-Munje Pact. "Note Ambedkar not our man."

(5) From, Mr. Laxman Sura Gohil, President, Mehgwal Sudharak Sabha "Support Rajah-Munje Pact" and "Disown Ambedkar and his London Pact."

Mahars Disown Ambedkar

(6) To Lord Lothian, From L. Gangawane, Secretary, Satara District Mahar Sangh, Satara District "Mahars wholeheartedly support Rajah-Munje Pact, disagree with Minority Pact in London, by Dr. Ambedkar. Trust in Rajah alone.

It is understood Mr. D.D. Gholap the first nominated member to Montford Council is advocating Joint Electorates.

(7) Mr. Shanakarrao Malharrao Patil, on behalf of Satara, Poona, Sholapur, Nasik, Khandesh, Ratnagiri, Thana Kolaba and Ahmednagar Associations of Chamars Tanners and Leather Workers "Support Rajah-Munje Pact. Disown Ambedkar and his London Pact."

(8) From Mr. Kale, to Lord Lothian, (Satara District Chamahrs) "Want Joint Electorates with adult Franchise, full confidence in Rajah.

Mr. Vithal Ranoji Ahireker to Lord Lothian, "Hairliea Chambahrs Samaj support Rajah-Munje Pact

(9) From Mr. K.P. Talegaokar to Lord Lothian "Chewli Hitawardh Samaj support Rajah-Munje Pact, Disown Ambedkar."

(10) From Mr. Sakharam Bhown Karjolkar, "Dabholi Chamabhara support Rajah-Munje Pact, Advocate adult Franchise for all."

(11) Mr. Gangaram Hanumantrao Pandirkar, "Rohidas Sewa Sangh support Rajah Munje Pact Disown Ambedkar and his London Pact."

(12) Mr. Ramchandra Balaram Deolekar, "Thana Untouchables support Rajah-Munje Pact."

(13) Mr. Shivram Sadanand Desai "Rohidas Social Club support Rajah-Munje Pact."

(14) From Mr. B.L. Deorukahar, "Rohidas Education Society support Rajah Munje Pact."

(15) Mr. Shankar Krishnaji Chandorkar, Member School Board, Kurla: "Depressed Classes of Kurla support Rajah Munje Pact."

(16) From Mr. Mahadeo Govind Khoker, "Anti-Untouchability Central Board support Rajah-Munje Pact."

(17) From Mr. Swalaram Gundaji Doifode, "Leather Workers Association support Rajah-Munje pact."

(18) Mr. Ananda Vithal Ahirekar, "Bombay Presidency Chambhars Central Committee support Rajah-Munje Pact."

(19) "Rohidas Samaj Hitavardhak support Rajah Munje Pact. Govind Borgharker Secretary."

(20) Mr. Murar Kara, President Rohit Samaj Bulsar "Depressed Classes Bulsar support Rajah-Munje Pact."

(21) Mr. Dewji Dala Bhai, President Rohit Samaj Kacholi Jalalpur:-

"Full support from D.C. Kacholi for Rajah-Munja Pact."

**

36. The Bombay Chronicle

Bombay

2-4-1932

THE FLOWING TIDE

The statement issued by Dr. Ambedkar, which is published in another column, disclosing private correspondence on the subject of electorates which took place between him and Messrs. Gawai and Jadhav respectively will not, we imagine, make much impression on the public. The object, of course, is to discredit the Rajah-Moonje Pact and the support it has received in the country. Dr. Ambedkar is audacious enough to assert that the Pact has been repudiated by the Depressed Classes all over India and that the Association is only a paper organisation. His first contention is so extravagant that it need not be seriously discussed. It is known that the Pact has received very wide and influential support. Depressed Classes institutions all over the country have declared their adhesion to it.

To cite only one case, the memorandum declaring for joint electorates, submitted to the Franchise Committee in Bombay by Mr. B. J. Deorukhkar and other local leaders of his community, was supported by 145 Associations and 5,000 members of the community. The Memorandum declared unreservedly for joint electorates. Only three days ago we published the wires sent to Lord Lothian by about twenty Depressed Class Associations of Bombay supporting the Rajah-Moonje Pact specifically. It is absurd for Dr. Ambedkar and his official friends to attempt to ignore this increasing support for joint electorates.

As regards the All-India Depressed Classes Association, which Dr. Ambedkar calls a paper Association, everybody knows that this body has been recognised for the last six or seven years as one of the largest, if not the largest, of All India organisations of the Depressed Classes, with a membership of about 40,000 persons. As for Mr. Rajah's connection with the Association, Mr. R. Gawai, one of its founders, stated at a meeting of the Franchise Committee at Delhi that since its formulation in 1925 Mr. Rajah has been yearly elected its President, though in 1926 Mr. Ambedkar's name was proposed but fell through for want of a seconder. Yet merely because Dr. Moonje, before concluding a Pact with Mr. Rajah attempted negotiations with Dr. Ambedkar, the latter childishly remarks: "Evidently" Dr. Moonje did not think Mr. Rajah the representative of the Depressed Classes to be negotiated with.

Dr. Ambedkar's publication of private correspondence will hardly serve any purpose beyond showing that he is indifferent to the honourable restrictions imposed on disclosure of private letters by the ethics of decent controversy. At the Delhi meeting of the Franchise Committee also he attempted to read a private letter he had received but Mr. Chintamani objected and the Chairman held up the objection. The principal letters now published by Dr. Ambedkar merely show that Mr. Gawai was strongly in favour of separate electorates even a few days before he accepted the Rajah-Moonje Pact. Change of views in politics is nothing uncommon among persons who are free to keep an open mind and are capable of keeping an open mind with regard to controversies. Dr. Ambedkar himself was strongly in favour of joint electorate before he changed his mind. He has now committed himself so far that he is not free to go back to his earlier convictions, cannot deny to others the freedom which he has himself exercised before. Much less is he entitled to question, as he does in his statement, "the *bonafides* of the change of view these persons have undergone." It is too late to stem the flowing tide of support for joint electorates from the Depressed Classes and it certainly cannot be done by the questionable methods employed by Dr. Ambedkar.

**

37. The Hindustan Times

Delhi

3-4-1932

Dr. Ambedkar's Propaganda
Lahore Citizens' Condemnation

Lahore, March 31.

To condemn the anti-nationalist and anti-Hindu Separatist propaganda amongst the untouchables being carried on by Dr. Ambedkar, Mr. Abdul Ghani, M.L.C., and others of the ilk, and in order to support the Rajah-Moonje Pact arrived at between the Hindu Mahasabha and the All-India Depressed Classes Association on the basis of the principle of joint electorates, a largely attended public meeting of the Hindu citizens of Lahore was held last evening in the Arya Samaj, Anarkali Hall, under the auspices of the Punjab Dalit Sewa Mission of the Arya Swarajya Sabha, Lahore, with Mr. Sukh Lal, a depressed class leader and a Municipal Commissioner of Karnal in the Chair.

The following resolutions were adopted: -

"This public meeting representing all shades of Hindu opinion declares that the unpatriotic attempts being made in certain circles at the vivisection of the Hindu body politic by pleading separate electorates for the untouchables is highly detrimental and suicidal to the interest of nationalism in the country and hence most emphatically condemns the highly objectionable propaganda of Dr. Ambedkar, which, on the face of it, is tantamount to playing into the hands of the enemies of the country, and which can only result in the perpetuation of the curse of untouchability in India.

This meeting gives its hearty support to the Moonje-Rajah Pact, which is based on the nationalist principle of joint electorates, and congratulates its authors for their statesmanship and foresight."

**

38. The Hindu
Madras
8-4-1932

Rajah-Moonje Pact

C.P. Depressed Class Association's Attitude

President Repudiates Previous Report

(From Our Own Correspondent)

Nagpur, April 7.

Mr. R.D. Wasnik, President of the Central Provinces Depressed Classes' Association, has sent the following telegram to the Chairman, Indian Franchise Committee: -

"I beg to inform you that the telegram sent to you in the name of the Central Provinces Depressed Classes' Association demanding separate electorate and repudiating the Rajah-Moonjee Pact, is totally false. The C.P. Depressed Classes' Association, of which I am the President, is the provincial branch of the All-India Depressed Classes' Association. The C.P. Depressed Classes' Association's Executive Committee meeting was not held on the 29th March. My Association fully supports the Rajah-Moonje Pact. Evidence was given by Mr. C.M. Thawre for joint electorate with reservation of seats on a population basis. The Mahars of Indora Basti, Nagpur, at their meeting have repudiated the Minorities Pact and advocated joint electorate. At the meetings of Depressed Classes held at Raipur and Tumsar, the Rajah-Moonje Pact and Mr. Thawre's evidence before the Indian Franchise Committee were supported.

**

39. The Statesman

Delhi

31-3-1932

Depressed Classes & Franchise

Inquiry "Breeze"

Witness's "I am not Being Accused"

Leaders of the Depressed Classes displayed conflicting views of the desire of the community for joint electorates at the meeting of the Indian Franchise Committee in New Delhi yesterday and there was a tense personal duel between Dr. Ambedkar and Rao Bahadur M.C. Rajah.

The first deputation to come before the Committee consisted of Rao Bahadur M.C. Rajah, President, Mr. Gavai and 12 others who appeared on behalf of the All-India Depressed Classes Association.

Answering Lord Lothian Rao Bahadur Rajah said that by Depressed Classes he meant those who were untouchables and also those who were not given access to common wells and common highways. They numbered 40,000 (typing error?) and were not admitted into Government service. In fact, there were rules and regulations in the Public Service Commission which hampered members of the Depressed Classes from getting appointments.

The disabilities of the Depressed Classes in northern India were not so great as of those in Southern India, but, witness added, that there was a noticeable change in the angle of vision even in South India.

"How?" asked the President, and Mr. Rajah proceeded to give instances. For example, he said, members of the Depressed Classes were now admitted without any complaint into Hindu restaurants. Then, there was the case of a member of the Committee (Rao Bahadur Srinivasan) having a Brahman priest officiating at a marriage in his house. Such a thing was inconceivable three years ago. Rao Bahadur Rajah hoped that in the course of a few years conditions in the south would come up to the level of conditions in north India.

15 Per Cent Enfranchised

Asked by the Chairman how he would work out a joint electorate with reservation of seats for Depressed Classes (from a purely administrative point of view), witness said he did not expect any difficulty, at all. There were Depressed Classes in each district and if the franchise now suggested was accepted there would be sufficient men enfranchised to claim at least one seat for each district in his own province. On the basis of the franchise he suggested there would be about 15 per cent of the population enfranchised. Those elected to provincial legislatures, district boards, taluk boards and union boards, could join into an electoral college for electing the required number for the Federal Legislature.

All India Body

The Chairman next questioned Rao Bahadur Rajah regarding the Depressed Classes Association. Witness stated that the membership totalled 40,000. It was started in 1925 with its headquarters at Nagpur. It was the only Depressed Class organization of an all-India character. As for meetings held in Delhi in February this year, witness explained that there was first a consultative meeting of members of the Working Committee of the Association and other principal leaders of the Depressed Classes community to discuss the Franchise Committee questionnaire and the Hindu Mahasabha's offer in respect of a joint electorate with reservation of seats. There were representatives from Bombay, Madras, U.P., the Punjab and C.P. The consensus of opinion at the meeting was in favour of a joint electorate with reservation of seats. Then there was the meeting of the Working Committee which endorsed that view. Swami Achutanand was a member of the Committee but did not attend, and therefore he would not be justified in saying that the committee did not pass a resolution supporting joint electorates.

The Memorandum submitted to the Committee had not been sent to any of the local organizations as there was no time, but was passed by the Working Committee in which there were representatives of almost all the provinces.

Dewan Bahadur Ramaswamy Mudaliar asked: With reference to local bodies can you say whether members of your own choice had been elected on the principle of joint electorate with reservation of seats for depressed classes?

Mr. Rajah: We not only obtained seats reserved for us, but also captured more seats.

Dewan Bahadur Ramaswami Mudaliar proceeded to question Mr. Muniswami, a member of the deputation, when Dr. Ambedkar objected, and the Chairman, while inclined to favour Dr. Ambedkar on the ground of want of time, allowed Dewan Bahadur Ramaswami Mudaliar to confine himself to a few questions. Mr. Muniswami explained as to what would be the position of the Adi Dravidas if they were classified separately.

Proceeding Mr. Rajah stated that the proposal for a joint electorate with reservation of seats for Depressed Classes was a recent one but when asked by Dewan Bahadur Ramaswami Mudaliar whether it was his view that the bulk of the Depressed Classes would support that policy, the President intervened and ruled the question out of order.

The witness did not share the view that if special representation was given to the Depressed Classes it would render unnecessary the special representation of Labour. He maintained that labour should get separate representation independent of what the Depressed Classes might get.

Asked whether he thought that in the present state of backwardness of the Depressed Classes there would be a sufficient number of men forthcoming in every province to fill the seats given on a population basis in all the provincial legislatures and in the Central Legislature, the Rao Bahadur said: You may not get men with university qualifications, but surely you can get scores of men of common sense who can follow debates in councils and exercise the vote rightly.

Answering Mr. Chintamani, Mr. Gavai stated that he has been working in the cause of the Depressed Classes for 25 years and gave evidence before the Southborough Committee. He formed the All-India Depressed Classes Association in 1925, since which year Rao Bahadur Rajah had been its president. In 1928, Dr. Ambedkar's name was proposed but fell through for want of a seconder. Dr. Ambedkar interjected: Thank you very much.

Dr. Ambedkar occupied 45 minutes in his cross-examination of the witnesses. He disproved the claims of two members of the deputation, one to be the editor of a newspaper and the other to be a member of Poona Municipality. He obtained from Mr. J. Handal the statement that his Association was started only a month ago. As for Mr. H.J. Khandekar, Dr. Ambedkar was told that the Mahar Youth League was not affiliated to the Depressed Classes Association and that he had come here as a member of the Association and not of the League.

Dr. Ambedkar then read a telegram from the Mahar Youth League repudiating the Rajah-Moonje Pact.

The witness: It is a bogus telegram. No meeting of the League could have been held with myself, its general secretary, away in Delhi and the Secretary of the League in hospital.

Dr. Ambedkar pulled out a private letter received by him, but Mr. Chintamani objected to the use of documents which had not been officially received by the Committee. The Chairman ruled that there was no general prohibition and that every letter should be treated as to relevancy on its own merits.

Rao Bahadur Rajah said that he could produce any number of letters but refrained from mentioning them.

In answer to Dr. Ambedkar, Rao Bahadur Rajah said that he could not give the names of all the members of the Working Committee of the Association but promised to send them later.

Dr. Ambedkar and Rao Bahadur Rajah then engaged in a prolonged duel over what actually happened at the consultative meeting on February 21 and at the meeting of the Working Committee on February 22. At one stage Dr. Ambedkar demanded answers in the form of a simple "yes" or "no", whereupon Rao Bahadur Rajah protested that he was not an accused before a third class magistrate.

Rao Bahadur Rajah emphasized that the proceedings of the consultative meeting, which supported joint electorates, should be read with the report of the Working Committee.

Dr. Ambedkar: Does your Association collect subscriptions?

Witness! We do not, as our community is poor but those who subscribe to our creed become members.

Sir Mohammad Yakub was told that the Depressed Classes wanted reservation of seats because they were not yet properly organized.

Mr. Chintamani questioned Rao Bahadur Rajah about the model answer which Dr. Ambedkar was reported to have sent to Mr. Gavai for submission to the Committee.

Rao Bahadur Rajah distributed several copies of the letter, Dr. Ambedkar observing that he was prepared to stand by it. Dr. Ambedkar observed that he merely told Mr. Gavai in that letter his views and did not suggest that he should adopt them.

Mr. Gavai: That is true.

Swami Achutanand and Mr. Baldeo Prasad Jaiwar also gave evidence on behalf of the All-India Depressed Classes Association. Referring to the memorandum submitted by Mr. G.A. Gavai the witnesses stated that the meeting referred to by Mr. Gavai as being held in Delhi on February 21 and 22 was not a meeting of the Working Committee of the Association. Moreover there were people present at the meeting who were not members of the Association. The meeting was not called to consider the questionnaire of the Franchise Committee but certain proposals of the Hindu Mahasabha. Witnesses further stated that the Association was always for separate electorates.

Swami Achutanand replying to the Chairman said that he did not understand the memorandum as he did not know English. Replying to Mr. Chintamani Mr. Baldeo Prasad said that he did not agree with the views expressed by Rao Bahadur M.C. Rajah. To Mr. Mudaliar he said that he was not aware whether at the Delhi meeting the question of separate or joint electorates was discussed.

**

040. The Statesman

Delhi

9-4-1932

Finding the Leader

Inevitably one consequence of the Lothian Committee's work is the accentuation of certain differences. When men cannot agree, every time they argue and disagree makes them more convinced that their own views are right and the others are wrong. Argument and discussion thicken the line between opinion and opinion. The world knows much more than it did about communal difficulties in India since the Round Table Conference dealt with them. The reason is not only that the London discussions were studied everywhere; the speakers themselves arrived at greater clearness and conviction about their own opinions in the process of preparing their speeches and answering questions across the table. It is probable that the minority communities learned much about their own needs from considering them afresh in relation to Mr. Gandhi's attitude to communal representation, and Dr. Ambedkar's popularity with his own people seems to have been considerably enhanced by the events of those few exciting days last November.

But, it has since been asserted, Dr. Ambedkar is not the accepted representative of his own class, which is the total of all that we generally call the depressed or backward classes. He was one of two selected to speak for them in London: had these classes been permitted to choose for themselves they would have chosen otherwise. Mr. Gandhi himself claimed in London that had it been a matter of voting the Untouchables would have elected him as their representative head of the poll, a statement at once strongly repudiated in India. When there is no numerical test by voting, when representatives are chosen by a kind of vague estimation of their standing and importance, rival claims can easily be set up. What has been made clear of late is that Dr. Ambedkar's position has been challenged in his own community, which is a "minority" of some 60 or 70 millions spread over most parts of India. Mr. Rajah, it is said, is the natural leader and his voice was heard in the recent Moonje-Rajah Pact. In other words the Depressed Classes want joint electorates though their spokesmen in London uncompromisingly identified themselves with separate electorates. The same claim has been made for Dr. Ansari. If he, Mr. Rajah and Mr. Gandhi are accepted as the spokesmen for Moslems, Backward Classes and Hindus then the case is established. India is unanimous for joint electorates and those who dissent, being of no particular importance, may be ignored by the British public and Parliament and Government.

Whether Dr. Ambedkar or Mr. Rajah speaks for them (there is no other claimant to the position) is for these classes themselves to decide. What they think others must accept, whether they like it or not, as a contribution to a complicated problem. So far as we can judge on what they have decided, Dr. Ambedkar's selection for the Round Table Conference was generally approved and his work in London applauded. Nor was it suspected that Mr. Rajah or anyone else of importance in the same community held other views about the proper method of representation. A statement recently published by Dr. Ambedkar has told the public more than it knew about the origin of the Moonje-Rajah Pact. Dr. Moonje, it appears, first approached Dr. Ambedkar with an offer of separate electorates for the Depressed Classes for five years, joint electorates afterwards. Failing to persuade him to an agreement he then approached Mr. Rajah and the All India Depressed Classes Association, an organization which despite its title seems unknown in Bengal, Bombay, Madras and some other Provinces and is said to have no impressive membership where it is found. We are told also that the Association has not empowered Mr. Rajah to bind himself in this way. There have been indecisive discussions, that is all. During the sittings of the Round table Conference Mr. Rajah (not a member) was certainly thought of as an advocate of special electorates, nor did he say anything to correct this impression in his personal memorandum submitted to the Lothian Committee. His change of faith would seem to have been recent and sudden. There are committees at work trying to learn what realities are in India as a preliminary to constitutional advance. They must decide between assertion and assertion, claim and claim. The diverse interests of the different communities are sufficiently embarrassing in themselves; when there is the additional complication of minorities within minorities their task becomes almost overwhelming. Do the Depressed Classes agree with Mr. Rajah? If so let them say so in no uncertain voice. It would be stupid to let a wrong opinion prevail without effort to correct it. As we read the signs, things are much as they were when the minorities combined to make their statement in London.

**

41. The Hindu
Madras
11-4-1932

Rajah-Moonje Pact
Mahar Youth League's Attitude
Legality of "Committee Meeting" Challenged
(From our own Correspondent)

Nagpur, April 10.

In a letter to the Press, Mr. H.J. Khandekar, General Secretary of the C.P. Mahar Youth League (Depressed Classes' Association) challenges the legality and bona fides of a meeting of the Executive Committee of the League held at Nagpur on the 28th of March. It may be mentioned here that at that meeting the Rajah—Moonje Pact was condemned and separate electorate with seats on a population basis, demanded for the Depressed Classes. A telegram to that effect was also sent to Lord Lothian on behalf of the League. Mr. Khandekar says: -

It appears that a meeting was called at Mr. Sakhre's house at Nagpur on the 28th March last in the evening. On that day, the President of the League was not in the station; one of the Assistant Secretaries was at Kamptee, and the other in the Mayo Hospital as an indoor patient. And the General Secretary had left Nagpur for Delhi that very morning. No proper notice was circulated to the members of the committee as required under the rules and regulations of the League. Mr. Sakhre, as Vice President notified a few members of the date and time of the meeting, but when the meeting was convened, it was found that there was no quorum Mr. Sakhre, thereupon, sent his friend Mr. Meshram in a motorcar to Gorewada to bring the President of the League. On being told that his presence was necessary at a dinner party at Nagpur, the President came along with Mr. Meshram, but when he was asked to preside over the meeting, he refused and declared it illegal. Mr. Sakhre still carried on the show, and finding that there was no quorum, he co-opted some of his friends as members of the Executive Committee then and there against the rules of the League. Before he had even been proposed to the chair, Mr. Sakhre occupied it and started work. This attitude was resented by some members of the executive who signified their protest by walking out of the meeting. Nothing daunted, Mr. Sakhre carried on and had resolutions of his own choice adopted. The resolutions were duly sent to the Press and wired to the Lothian Committee. In giving evidence before the Franchise Committee at Delhi on the 30th March I, as the General Secretary, had to repudiate this telegram as bogus.

I do not know what was Mr. Sakhre's motive in holding a meeting of this kind in haste. Till then he had never signed any notice (...cannot be read).

**

42. The Statesman

Delhi

17-4-1932

Rejected Proposal

Depressed Class Vote Against Pact

(From a Correspondent)

Raniket, April 16.

A Depressed Class mass meeting was held at Garur (Almora, Kumain), when full confidence in Dr. Ambedkar was voiced and the pact proposal of Mr. Rajah and the Mahasabhaites was rejected.

**

43. The Hindu

Madras

19-4-1932

In a communication which we publish elsewhere, Mr. M.C. Rajah gives an illuminating analysis of the number of seats in the various legislatures which the members of his community stand to secure under the various schemes hitherto propounded for the representation of the depressed classes. It shows that under the so-called Minorities Pact of the Round Table Conference—to which the Ambedkar-Srinivasan group of the depressed classes has made itself a party—the depressed classes stand to get considerably less than what the Congress has conceded as their due, namely, seats in proportion to their population. Under that scheme, only in two provinces—Bombay and Madras—do they get a small weightage. Of the other provinces, in two they get seats roughly in proportion to population, but in the rest, the four important provinces of Bengal, the Punjab, the United Provinces and the Central Provinces, they secure representation which is below their numerical strength. It is significant also that if the recommendations of the local Provincial Franchise Committees and the Provincial Governments are accepted, the depressed classes will get something considerably less than what their numerical strength warrants. When Mr. Srinivasan expected 40 seats in a Council of 200 in Madras under the Minorities Pact, the Local Government has recommended but 18 seats out of 210 seats! Therein lies the difference between the official blessed separate electorate schemes and the other schemes. Thus, under the joint electorates scheme of Messrs Rajah and Moonje, the depressed classes get not only what they would on a strictly population basis, but also probably something more immediately and possibly a good deal more in course of time. We hope that the members of the depressed classes will study the communication with care and realise that their best interests will be served, under a system, not of separate electorates which is a device calculated to secure weightage for more favoured communities at their expense, but of joint electorates which guarantees them seats *pro rata* to their numerical strength with opportunities of securing more because of the freedom to contest as many seats as they choose.

**

44. The Hindustan Times
Delhi
21-4-1932

(From Our Correspondent)

Nagpur, April 18.

In the course of a statement to the Press, Mr. G.M. Thawre, Assistant General Secretary, All-India Depressed Classes Association, says: -

I have received a number of letters asking the reason why we demand joint electorate, and notable persons have already expressed their approval of the system of joint electorate.

Ever since the year 1919 right up to the end of the year 1931, we ourselves were in favour of separate electorate, but have now realised the definite ruin in future in clinging fast to it. We have, therefore, changed our views.

The Central Provinces Government has recommended only 10 seats for the Depressed Classes and Labour combined, when according to our population proportion we are entitled to 22 seats. The percentage of Moslems is only 4, and yet they get 10 seats. That is the justice done to us.

Yet, curiously enough, R.B. Shrinivasan, in collaboration with Dr. Ambedkar, proposed at the R.T.C. a reduction of seats for the Depressed Classes in other provincial Councils and a consequent increase in the Bombay and Madras Councils.

Change in Views

We have been charged with having changed our views so soon as that. That truly is not so. It took us a full decade to get rid of those old conservative ideas, and certainly not without reason. The cardinal reason for such a change is that the Prime Minister, in this speech at the R.T.C., has already spoken of the grant of provincial autonomy.

There is a world of difference between the system as it obtains today and the proposed provincial autonomy. Under the present system the whole administration rests in the hands of Englishmen, and the Government can safely and unscrupulously give a go bye to all resolutions and recommendations of the Council.

This system will not obtain under the proposed provincial autonomy, under which the reins of Government would be in the hands of the majority party, as we find at present in the British Parliament.

Joint Action with Hindus

The Hindus are in an over-whelming majority in the provinces and even if the minority communities combine according to the pact of Dr. Ambedkar, they will not be able to overcome the Hindus majority. So the Depressed Classes, if they separate from the Hindus will not be able to do anything in the legislatures.

If we are really desirous of promoting the cause of our community (...cannot be read) object is to remove untouchability. If we become a distinct community, it will not only not remove untouchability, but will help to strengthen the feeling of animosity and heart-burning among untouchable and caste Hindus.

It has been said that under the joint electorate system only the favourite of the Hindus will be returned, but the same may be said with equal propriety or impropriety of the separate electorates. Rao Bahadur M.C. Rajah has given his experience in the Madras Presidency in his letter to the *Times of India* of March 25, 1932.

Madras Experience

The Non-Brahmin Party of Madras demanded separate electorate in 1919. They did not get it. Instead they were given joint electorate with some reserved seats. The result is that the Non-Brahmins lost nothing at all. On the contrary, it has made the Justice party dominant.

The same can be said of the Central Provinces. To-day, under the system of joint electorates, the Democratic Party, which is in all a party of Non-Brahmins, rules supreme in the local Council, and the efforts of the combined group of the Nationalists and people's parties to dethrone it have proved more than once unsuccessful.

The Moslem President of our Council was elected with the help of the Democratic Party. What could the seven Moslem members have done without their support. The Lucknow pact gives Moslems more seats than they really are entitled to. Why should we not make use of the offer of the Hindu Maha Sabha to our advantage?

Advantage

It is for these advantages that my association has changed its views. We are fully convinced that the separate electorate system is not profitable and hence not suitable. It is suicidal and highly prejudicial to our interests. Joint electorate is beneficial and therein alone lies our political salvation.

The Moslems entered into a Pact with the Indian National Congress at Lucknow, Dr. Ambedkar effected a Pact in England with the minority communities, and Rao Bahadur Rajah entered into an agreement with Dr.

Moonje at New Delhi. Of these three Pacts, the New Delhi Pact alone is perfect and judicious.

Dr. Ambedkar's Pact may be beneficial from the Moslem point of view, but it helps the Depressed Classes in no way. Dr. Ambedkar may be qualified man, but he is a poor politician. The Rajah-Moonje Pact seems to me a sovereign balm for the ailment of the Depressed (...cannot be read).

**

45. The Times of India

Bombay

25-4-1932

Shoe Flung At President
Uproar At Meeting
Rajah-Moonje Pact Repudiated

(From our own correspondent)

Nagpur, April 22.

Uproarious scenes were witnessed this evening at a meeting of the Depressed Classes this evening presided over by Mr. Khandekar. The President was continuously heckled and a shoe was flung at him by someone in the meeting.

The meeting was of protagonists of the Rajah-Moonje Pact and was held in the Town Hall.

At the outset Mr. Tularam Sakhre M.L.C., demanded that the meeting should not merely listen to speeches but that a resolution for or against joint electorates should be put to the meeting and votes taken.

The Chairman declined to allow this. Thereupon Mr. Sakhre held a separate meeting close by at which resolutions supporting Dr. Ambedkar and separate electorates and condemning the Rajah-Moonje Pact were carried.

The meeting in the Town Hall was dissolved amidst great confusion. The City Superintendent of Police, Mr. Parmeshwar Dayal was present at the meeting with a party of police and endeavoured to maintain order.

**

46. The Hindustan Times

Delhi

1-5-1932

Joint Electorates Necessary
Mr. Rajah Explains
Advantages of Pact With Hindu Sabha

Madras, April 27.

Rao Bahadur M.C. Rajah, M.L.A., in the course of a statement further explaining the advantages to the Depressed Classes of the Rajah-Moonje Pact, says: -

"It is deplorable that members of our community, of whom better things are expected should either blindly or willfully support the surrenders which the Depressed Classes delegates have made before other communities at the Round Table Conference, and that too at a time when the future of the community is hanging in the balance, and a false step taken at the present moment will perpetuate in the new condition of things the subordinate, if not the servile, place we have hitherto been occupying in the body politic of India."

Separate Electorates

He adds: "Separate Electorates would have been a kind of safeguard under Diarchy in which our representatives joining with the Government section might have secured for us what we wanted.

"But under Provincial Autonomy our aim should be to secure in a Joint Electorate a sufficiently large number of seats for our community. This can be done by means of Reservation granted to us by Statute, with liberty to contest non-reserved seats and by so organising ourselves as to capture additional seats over and above the reserved seats."

Concluding he says: "Under Provincial Autonomy if we returned through Separate Electorates, even if we form a compact body, which as I have said is doubtful, we shall always have to play a second fiddle to one or another party, and never be an integral part of any party, with an opportunity which will come sooner or later of sharing in the Government of the Province.

Scope for Constructive Work

"Under Provincial Autonomy such identification with the party which comes out victorious in a general electorate is absolutely essential, not merely for preventing other communities from doing harm to us, but for constructive work which will elevate us and place us on a level with the most cultured and influential community in the country."

It is after considering all these things and discussing the matter from all points of view and consulting some of the wisest and far-seeing men in the country, both in the North and in the South, who wish well of our community and who have laboured for our uplift in the past, and above all, after discussing the matter for days and nights together with the leaders of our community in different provinces, that, I have come to the conclusion that we should cast our lot with the general community who, after all that is said and done, hold the reins of power in their hands. With them we sink or rise, and our future lies in identification with them. Our progress is theirs, and their progress is ours."—A.P.I.

**

47. The Leader
Allahabad
2-5-1932

Support to Rajah-Moonje Pact

Ratnagiri, April 27

Mr. V. Surve, M.L.C., (Ratnagiri) interviewed said that he supported the Rajah-Moonje Pact and believed that the best interests of the so-called untouchables could be far more effectively served by reservation of seats with joint electorates than by separate electorates. He yielded to none in condemning the evils of untouchability and said that the very fact that the Ratnagiri Hindu Sabha, which was one of the most active and influential Hindu organizations in the district, was leaving no stone unturned to uproot this evil and had already achieved such striking success, showed that influential Hindu opinion in his district was determined to wipe out the curse of untouchability. He was glad to see that an overwhelming majority of the untouchables was far-sighted and patriotic enough to come forward to support the Rajah-Moonje Pact and he hoped that even Dr. Ambedkar would soon be converted and he would become a staunch supporter of joint electorates. In conclusion he reiterated his view that joint electorates with reservation of seats would effectively safeguard the special interests of the untouchables and would enable them to reap the benefits of a consolidated and united Hindu community.

**

48. The Hindustan Times

Delhi

3-5-32

Minorities Pacts Condemned

Depressed Classes Conference

Nagpur, May 1.

A conference of the Depressed Classes was held at Dakram Sukari in the Bhandara District under the presidency of Mr. Tulsi Ram Patel of Falchur. About 5000 people from all districts in the Central Provinces and Berar attended. It condemned the interference of the Bombay government in the Nasik Satyagraha, offered by the depressed classes and requested the C.P. Government to fix a commission for the *malguzars* on collections from *abadi* lands. The conference also condemned the Minority Pact of Dr. Ambedkar and supported the Rajah-Moonje-Pact. Mr. S.V. Dahat who had opposed the last resolution ultimately voted for it on the very convincing explanations given by Messrs. Khandekar and Godghate as to the advantages of the one and the disadvantage of the other.

**

49. The Statesman

Delhi

10-5-1932

Repudiated

Depressed Classes and Mr. Rajah

Nagpur, May 9.

Rao Bahadur Rajah's claim to leadership was repudiated and confidence expressed in Dr. Ambedkar at the second session of the All-India Depressed Classes Congress held at Kamptee.

About 200 delegates from all parts of India except Assam, with 1,000 local delegates, including women, attended the Congress.

Rao Sahib Muniswamy Pillay of Madras presided.

Mr. Hardas, chairman of the reception committee, in welcoming the delegates, said that the so-called National Congress under the leadership of Mr. Gandhi had been trying its utmost to mislead the Depressed Classes and harm their interest within and without the country whenever they could. Controversy about joint versus separate electorates had been advanced so far that they could not in any circumstances accept joint electorates. Their position was that with a joint electorate they died and with a separate electorate they lived.

"Ugly Game"

In the course of his speech Mr. Pillay said: -

"Meager as our representation was at the Round Table Conference, we are glad that our spokesman, Dr. Ambedkar, discharged his duties in a most magnificent manner. By his ability and wisdom he raised the Depressed Classes in the estimation of others. At the Round Table Conference the claims of the Depressed Classes were most vehemently opposed by the representatives of the caste-Hindus. They claimed that the Congress and Mr. Gandhi represented the Depressed Classes more than Dr. Ambedkar and asserted that the majority of the Depressed Classes were opposed to special protection and special representation. When this most preposterous claim and most unwarranted and mischievous assertion of the Congress were challenged by Dr. Ambedkar, what was it that the Congressmen did in this country? They got hold of a few hirelings and dupes here and there, formed mushroom associations and through these persons who have neither any stake in society nor any following in the community, messages were sent to England expressing lack of confidence in Dr. Ambedkar. And these messages were printed in big letters by the Nationalist Press and wide publicity given to them. If half-a-dozen misguided members of the Depressed Classes could play puppets in the hands of the Congressmen and they raised a cry then the columns of the Nationalist Press contained bold head lines, such as 'Bombay's united stand against Dr. Ambedkar.' 'Ambedkar repudiated by the Depressed Classes.' 'Mahatma Gandhi the representative of the Depressed Classes, not Dr. Ambedkar.'

"While political jugglery of this kind was going on under the patronage of the Congress and the Hindu Mahasabha, responsible leaders of the community all over India including Gujarat where Mahatma Gandhi is the strongest, sent 54 telegrams and several other representations to Dr. Ambedkar expressing their confidence in him and supporting his demands. Curiously enough most of these things were suppressed by the Nationalist Press. I have now to express my emphatic condemnation of the most ugly game played by the Congressmen in this respect and to tell them that things like these are highly unworthy of persons of honest ways. In spite of the tremendous power and the unlimited resources of the Congress to denounce him, Dr. Ambedkar is our most trusted and honoured leader. Him alone do we recognize as entitled to speak on our behalf at the Round Table Conference.

Difference of Method

"The Depressed Classes have been accused of treason against the political progress of India. I may tell our critics very plainly that the Depressed Classes are not at all opposed to the political freedom of India. Our differences with the rest of our countrymen are in the question of the method and the time of achieving this freedom for India. What we are opposed to is that kind of political freedom now demanded by our countrymen, namely, a political freedom which gives the majority communities all the coveted facilities to oppress the Depressed Classes unquestioned and unresisted by others. India should now be given a system of Self-Government, not Independence, in which political power will be the common property of all peoples and not the exclusive monopoly of the privileged classes and powerful communities who, on account of their wealth, education and social standing form a powerful aristocracy of their own. It is only such a system that will give a sense of security to the minority communities, and it is only such a sense of security that will make them consent to the grant of political power for India.

It is for the right to share political power that we want special representation in the legislatures according to the strength of our population.

Distrust of Caste-Hindus

"We want special representation so that we may prevent the chances of political power being used by the caste people against us. We want special representation so that the authorities of the country may have the means of studying our affairs and our wants and so that they may give us what we want in common with others. We do not want special representation for any other purpose. The Depressed Classes do not trust the caste-Hindus. I do not want to make a secret of this fact. I want to tell Mr. Gandhi, his Congress, his admirers everywhere and the whole world that we of the Depressed Classes are not prepared to trust the caste Hindus and that our experiences in the past and to-day do not justify any such trust from us in their honesty and consistency. By resisting our claim for special representation we are asked to trust in the promises of a few political leaders in the country.

No Magic Wand

"They say that when they get Swaraj they will get rid of social oppressions as if by the touch of the magic wand. What is the guarantee that these big leaders of the Hindu community will continue to be leaders when they actually try for the removal of caste barriers? Have not these people been talking of the removal of untouchability and such things so long a time and what is it that they have so far achieved apart from raising some little dust in their days? The passion for untouchability and for using it against the Depressed Classes is as dear to the caste-Hindus as life itself. To think that the caste-Hindus will part with it unless at the formidable pressure of the Depressed Classes themselves, is nothing but in idle dream. I challenge Mr. Gandhi to contest any elections in the country on the mere issue of untouchability and get a majority of him. Or I would ask him to take a referendum of the caste-people on the issue of untouchability and show to the world that he gets the majority of votes. It should by remembered that the great Mahatma, high and mighty as he is, has not been able to take the Depressed Classes into any of the Caste-Hindu temples in the country. It is significant that during his historic march to Dandi for salt satyagraha in a certain village, he was not allowed the village *choultry* for the simple reason that there was a member of the Depressed Classes with him. When Mr. Gandhi has not been able to do any of these things and when he is aware of all these things, his declarations at the Round Table Conference that untouchability will disappear with the advent of Swaraj and that the Depressed Classes will not require special representation as there will be no need for it are wanting in honesty and veracity.

"Bar Sinister"

"It is said that the claim of the Depressed Classes for special representation means the bar sinister and that it can only serve to perpetuate untouchability. I say that it is not at all our intention to perpetuate the bar sinister. We do not want to remain untouchables in perpetuity even though Mr. Gandhi's arguments may tend to make us so. We only want to function as a separate community for political purposes. We are not responsible for it. If this position creates a division in the Hindu fold we are not to blame for it. Let the caste- Hindus remove all the circumstances that make us suspect them and let conditions in India be such that every man and woman may enjoy his or her elementary rights of citizenship unprevented by others. Let all the existing divisions in Hinduism disappear and let the Hindu community become one homogeneous society without divisions of caste. It is then the time for the Depressed Classes not to have separate representation in the legislatures.

"I am unable to find an iota of generosity towards us in the efforts of the caste-Hindus to resist this special representation. It is all for the advantage and the interests of the caste Hindus themselves. The very excessive keenness and anxiety that characterize the struggles of the caste-Hindus to oppose special representation for the Depressed Classes are in themselves the strongest proof for it. The tenacious spirit of the Moslems in demanding their 14 points and particularly for statutory Moslem majorities in Bengal and the Punjab has terrified the Hindus and they want to strengthen their own positions at any cost. They find that special representation for the Depressed Classes will reduce their own strength in the councils and they will be reduced to a position of impotency and humiliation.

"It was some consolation to us that in spite of the opposition of the communal Hindus our demands were supported by the Moslems and other minorities. All honour to them for this."

Interrupters Fare Badly

During Saturday's rowdy scenes at Nagpur railway station when Dr. Ambedkar arrived, black-flaggers were set upon and Mr. Thaware, one of the staunchest supporters of the Rajah-Moonje Pact, had his lip cut open by a soda water bottle hurled at him and a friend of his, Mr. Mate, is alleged to have had his hand injured with a knife.

There was an unpleasant incident just before the Congress opened in the evening. Mr. Hardas, chairman of the reception committee had barely begun reading his welcome when Messrs. Rajbhoj and Patil, two delegates from Poona, challenged the legality and the representative character of the Congress. Half a dozen volunteers immediately fell upon them and Mr. Rajbhoj was handled very roughly. He later made a second attempt to address the gathering, but was hit from behind and fell down. Mr. Sakhre, vice-president of the reception committee, and the City Magistrate of Nagpur, came to Mr. Rajbhoj's rescue and led him and his two friends out of the *pandal*. Mr. Rajbhoj had to be taken to hospital.

**

50. The Leader
Allahabad
11-5-1932

Depressed Classes Conference
Pandemonium And Scuffle In Pandal
Conference Boycotted by Rajah-Moonje Pact Supporters
Several Resolutions Adopted
Black Flag Demonstration Against Dr. Ambedkar At Station

(From Our Correspondent)

Nagpur, May 7.

"The controversy about joint *vs.* separate electorates has been advanced so far that we cannot in any circumstances accept joint electorates. Now our position is such that with joint electorate we die and with separate electorate we live." In these words Mr. L.N. Hardas, editor of the *Maharatha,* Kamptee, and the chairman of the reception committee, welcomed the president and the delegates of the second session of the All-India Depressed Classes Conference which after many postponements was held this evening at Kamptee under the presidency of Rao Saheb Muniswamy Pillay, M.L.C., of Madras. About 100 delegates from all the provinces, except Assam and about 100 local delegates and a large number of visitors including some women attended the conference.

A large contingent of police with *lathis* was present both outside and inside the *pandal* to avert any disturbance.

When the chairman of the reception committee began to address, Mr. Raj Bhoj, editor of the *Dhalitha Bandhu*, and Mr. Shanker Rao Patil of Poona, advocates of joint electorates, questioned the legality of the Conference and wished to put some questions. This provoked the separationists who rushed on them and a pandemonium reigned for about half an hour and ultimately the exponents of joint electorates were forcibly removed outside the pandal. The timely intervention of the police eased the situation.

Rao Saheb Muniswamy Pillay, the president, then delivered the presidential address, in the course of which he advocated the utility and advantages of separate electorates to the depressed classes in the constitution and derided Mahatma Gandhi and the Indian National Congress.

Pandemonium Again

Oppostionists Not Allowed to Speak

(From Our Correspondent)

Nagpur, May 9.

Once again pandemonium reigned supreme at the meeting of the All India Depressed Classes Conference at Kamptee yesterday. While a resolution was being discussed some advocates of joint electorate made repeated requests to the president to afford them an opportunity of placing their views before the conference. The president refused to allow them to speak, remarking, it is alleged, that they were hirelings of the castemen. Many attempts were made by the separatists to rush on the oppositionists and the situation would have become serious but for the timely intervention of the police.

The fact that the advocates of joint electorates were refused permission to speak shows that the separatists were afraid of division in the conference if they were allowed to address it. Dr. Ambedkar was conspicuous by his silence. The conference adopted resolutions, among others, supporting the Minority Pact as containing the irreducible minimum demands of the depressed classes and claiming representation according to it, repudiating the Rajah-Moonje Pact, protesting against the inadequate representation given to the depressed classes at the Round Table Conference and urging greater representation on it, expressing loyalty to King-Emperor, condemning the terrorist movement in the country, regretting the policy of the Government in ignoring the cooperation of the depressed classes, claiming special facilities for the depressed classes in the Punjab Legislative Council, demanding representation on all local self-governing bodies on a population basis, supporting the temple entry Satyagraha at Nasik, urging the Government to afford special facilities for 'depressed classes' education and demanding depressed class woman suffrage for all local self-governing bodies and legislatures.

With the concluding speech of Rao Saheb Muniswamy Pillay, the president, the conference concluded its second session. The next session of the conference was invited to Calcutta.

(Associated Press)

Nagpur, May 7

The second session of the All India Depressed Classes Conference commenced today at Kamptee under the presidentship of Rai Sahib Muniswamy Pillay, M.L.C., from Madras. As anticipated the holding of the conference was the cause of some amount of trouble. In the morning when Dr. Ambedkar arrived from Bombay he was accorded a reception by his supporters, while a small group favouring joint electorates gathered at the Nagpur railway station to show black flags to him. This was the signal for trouble.

The black-flaggers were set upon and Mr. Thaware, one of the staunchest supporters of the Rajah-Moonje Pact, had his lip cut open by a soda water bottle hurled at him and a friend of his, Mr. Mate, is alleged to have had his hand injured by a knife. Messrs Mate, Gorghate and four others of the Rajah group were taken into police custody and removed from the railway station.

Nothing more untoward happened in the morning but there was an unpleasant incident just before the conference opened in the evening.

Mr. Hardas, chairman of the reception committee, had barely begun reading his welcome address when Messrs Rajbhoj and Patil, two of the delegates from Poona, challenged the legality and the representative character of the conference. Half a dozen volunteers immediately fell upon them and Mr. Rajbhoj was handled very roughly. Shortly after Mr. Rajbhoj made a second attempt to address the gathering and got hit from behind and fell down.

Mr. Sakhre, vice-president of the reception committee, and the city magistrate of Nagpur, who was present on the spot, both came to Mr. Rajbhoj's rescue and led him and his two friends out of the *pandal*. Mr. Rajbhoj had to be taken to hospital. But for these few delegates from outside today's session of the conference was scrupulously boycotted by the supporters of the Rajah-Moonje Pact.

The conference had attracted about 30 delegates from outside Nagpur, four coming from Bengal, five from the Punjab, seven from the United Provinces, four each from Bombay and Madras and one from Bihar. Nearly 1,500 Mahars of Nagpur and Kamptee and nearly 200 ladies were present. Both the Empress and Model mills were picketed and a large number of labourers absented themselves to attend the Kamptee conference.

Mr. Hardas, in his welcome address, said that the National Congress was trying to mislead the depressed classes and harm their interests, and its sister organization, the Hindu Mahasabha, had virtually declared war against them. 'We have to deal with them very cautiously. Joint electorates would amount to ruination of the depressed classes. We cannot in any circumstances accept joint electorates.'

Rai Sahib Muniswamy Pillay the president, said that the depressed classes had developed sufficient consciousness to assert their political rights and to feel in terms of nationalism consistently with their safety and security. He paid eloquent tributes to Dr. Ambedkar for the magnificent manner in which he had presented the case of the depressed classes at the Round Table Conference and said that Dr. Ambedkar's importance would not be belittled by any propaganda against him by interested press. The depressed classes, he asserted, had no faith in the Congress leaders. They must needs have separate electorates and special representation.

Resolutions Adopted

Nagpur, May 8.

Today's meeting brought to a termination the second session of the All-India Depressed Classes Conference. The conference adopted 12 resolutions, one of which supported Dr. Ambedkar's Minorities Pact and another emphatically repudiated the Rajah-Moonje Pact.

Today's session was attended by 12 men from the Rajah group who wanted to oppose both these resolutions. On each occasion there was an uproar and a minor scuffle but the police promptly checked any further spread of trouble. Mr. Khandekar and his friends who wanted to speak against these resolutions were not permitted to do so, but were asked to record their votes. Mr. Khandekar and the party left the *pandal* before the meeting was over.

The conveners of the conference and Dr. Ambedkar himself attempted during the night to persuade Messrs. Gavai, Thaware, Khandekar, Gorghate and other leaders of the opposition to come and take part in the subjects committee deliberations, but their attempts proved futile, the oppositionists maintaining that their organization, namely, the All-India Depressed Classes Association had not given them the necessary sanction to attend the Kamptee Conference. In view of this non-cooperating attitude the conveners of the Conference decided not to give Mr. Khandekar and his friends any opportunity to address the open session today.

All the 12 resolutions were therefore adopted without opposition. The resolution supporting the R.T.C. Minorities Pact was moved by Mr. Mallick from Bengal and comprised several clauses, stating *inter alia* that the Minorities Pact contained the irreducible minimum of the demands of the depressed classes who retained their right to any action they deemed fit in case their demands as embodied in the pact were not granted to the extent and in the manner specified therein. The Government was also warned to use caution in accepting the estimates regarding the numerical strength of the depressed classes in view of the fact that caste Hindus were making frantic efforts to reduce the number of the depressed classes in order to deprive them of their due share of representation in the legislatures. The resolution was supported by Mrs. Ogale.

The conference adopted several resolutions strongly condemning the terrorist movement, particularly the dastardly outrage on the life of the Midnapore magistrate, as also the civil disobedience movement. The conference expressed great appreciation of the services rendered by Dr. Ambedkar and Rao Bahadur R. Sreenivasan at the London Round Table Conference for the depressed classes and emphatically protested against the inadequate representation given to the depressed classes at the Round Table Conference.

The conference also urged that the depressed classes should have representation on the population basis in all local bodies and adequate funds should be set apart in the central budget for the promotion of higher education among them.

**

51. The Leader
Allahabad
12-5-1932

Not A Representative Body
So-called Depressed Classes Congress
How Resolutions Were Passed
Real Opinion Suppressed

Nagpur, May 10.

Mr. G.A. Gavai, general secretary of the All-India Depressed Classes Association, has issued the following to the press: -

The All-India Depressed Classes Association as a body could not and did not join the second session of the so-called All-India Depressed Classes Congress, a rival body, started by Dr. Ambedkar. We asserted and still assert that the majority of the depressed classes are for the Rajah-Moonje Pact. The fact that Mr. Khandekar and others were not allowed to address the audience in opposition to the Minority Pact and in support of the Rajah-Moonje Pact and that these two resolutions were declared passed without being put to the vote, in spite of loud demands from the delegates for a poll and that several hundred delegates left the pandal in a body by way of protest, shows that the decision of the Congress does not represent the real opinion of the depressed classes. The All-India Depressed Classes Association, therefore, proposes soon to hold an All-India Depressed Classes Conference at some central place to record the real opinion of the depressed classes on these two pacts.

**

52. The Tribune

Lahore

25-6-32

Mr. Rajah Suddenly Taken Ill

"Depressed" Classes Conference Postponed

Bombay, June 23.

Due to the sudden illness of Mr. M.C. Rajah, president-elect of the All-India Depressed Classes Conference, announced to be held in Bombay on June 16 the reception committee has postponed the Conference to a date in July, so as to enable Mr. Rajah to preside.

**

53. The Eastern Times

Lahore

12-7-1932

Bombay, Sunday.

The 10th session of the All-India Depressed Classes Conference concluded this evening after passing a series of resolutions. The first, which stated that the conference was of opinion that true interests of the depressed classes so far as their relation in political administration was concerned could best be promoted only by means of joint electorates with reservation of seats on their population basis in all the legislatures and in pursuance of that conviction accepted unreservedly the Rajah-Moonjee Pact which embodied that principle.

Effective Safeguards

The second resolution urged upon the British Cabinet the desirability of including proper effective directions for securing effective representation to the depressed classes by means of an instrument of instructions to the Governor General and Governors.

The third resolution repudiated the London Minority pact while the fourth urged unity in the ranks of the depressed classes.

The fifth resolution demanded age limit of qualification instead of educational and property qualifications for franchise.

The sixth resolution urged the Government to take fresh census of depressed classes and the seventh deputed Mr. M.C. Rajah to go to England in order to develop a sound public opinion.

Another resolution expressing loyalty to the Crown was moved from the chair and unanimously passed.

Presidential Address

According to an earlier message the Conference met on Sunday, Rao Bahadur M.C. Rajah presiding. Only 200 delegates were present. Sir Chunnilal Mehta, Bulabhai Desai, and Miraben also attended.

It is stated that separatists went to Victoria Terminus to greet Mr. M.C. Rajah, President of the Conference with black flags, but they were forestalled by the organisers of the Conference at whose instance the President detrained at Thana station and motored to Bombay.

Mr. M.C. Rajah in the course of his presidential address examined at length the attitude of Dr. Ambedkar, Rao Bahadur Srinivasan and Munuswami Pillay, President of the Depressed Classes Conference held at Kamptee on the question of joint versus separate electorates. Continuing

Mr. Rajah said: "If our men in the Councils become members of the Government they can do so only by being members of one or the other of the parties which contest seats in general constituency under the system of joint electorates." Mr. Rajah said that they considered the invitation of the Hindu Mahasabha to join them for work on a common platform and do away with untouchability as an earnest attempt of caste Hindus to remove untouchability.

Mr. Rajah added that after a prolonged discussion he had come to the conclusion that they should cast their lot with the general community who after all had said and done to hold the reins of power with them. "We sink or rise together and our future lies in identification with them." Mr. Rajah stated that he, on the whole, was satisfied with the Lothian Committees report with reference to the depressed classes and hoped His Majesty Government will soon accept its recommendations regarding depressed classes. A.P.I.

**

Section IV
Towards Poona Pact
Speeches and Letters

54. Speech delivered in the Legislative Assembly on 13 September 1932, by M. C. Rajah

Never in the annals of the history of India has the issue of the Depressed Classes assumed importance as it has today, and for this we of the Depressed Classes must forever be grateful to Mahatma Gandhi. He has told the world, in words which cannot be mistaken, that our regeneration is the fundamental aim of his life. If world conscience cannot be roused even now to the realization of the position of the Depressed Classes, then we can only conclude that all instincts of humanity are dead in the world today. Let me remind the House that ours is an all-India problem and not confined to some provinces as it is in the case of Muslims and Sikhs. I have heard it often repeated that the Muslim claim and the Sikh claim to special consideration is because they are martial races. So have we been in the ancient history of India. If they claim that they have been rulers in this country, so have we been in the ancient time. But, sir, what we claim is that we have in addition been the most law-abiding and loyal citizens even when social laws degraded us to a position of untouchability. We never took law into our hands, and depended upon the moral conscience of our countrymen being roused to a realization of the grave injustice and inhumanity practiced against us.

The question before the House is the situation created by Mahatma Gandhi opposing the grant of communal electorates to the Depressed Classes. I am sure there is no honorable member in this House who will not regret that circumstances should have forced such a great personality to take a vow to play on his life, but sir, the correspondence shows that Government had enough warning. If they did not attach full important to our considered views expressed in our conferences and in the Rajah-Moonje Pact I had signed with the president of Hindu Mahasabha, they should have taken at least the grave warning given by Mahatma Gandhi and desisted from the course of creating separate electorates. Sir, the situation as it confronts us today is as follows:

The British Government have given their communal decision. They declare that it shall hold good for 20 years in respect of the Depressed Classes, unless there is unanimous request made before the constitution is framed or ten years after the constitution has worked. I wonder what is meant by unanimous request? Has in the political history of any country such literal unanimity ever been attained on any issue? Is the British Government sure that Britishers are unanimous in giving India a further measure of responsibility? Is even the National Government sure that Conservatives as a whole back its Indian policy? This condition of unanimity is thus a dodge to keep us perpetually divided. I claim that my community is already in favour of common electorates, and I will prove my contention by a few quotations.

You all know that British Government sent two delegates to represent the Depressed Classes at the Round Table Conference, *viz.,* Dr. Ambedkar and Rao Bahadur Srinivasan. Dr. Ambedkar presented the case of the Depressed Classes in Bombay before the Simon Commission and he presented a statement of his Sabha where he pleaded for joint electorates. As regards Rao Bahadur Srinivasan, when he appeared before the Simon Commission in Madras, to a question put by a member of the Commission, whether he wanted separate electorates for the Depressed Classes, he said, "Not at present," and his reasons were: "our people are not yet advanced to have separate electorates. Unless you give adult franchise, the Depressed Classes should have no separate electorates." This was in 1929. When he went to the first R. T. C., the Depressed Classes' Federation of Madras, of which he is the president, passed a resolution supporting joint electorates and giving him that mandate for being placed before the R. T. C.

In this connection let me tell the House that even Dr. Ambedkar demanded joint electorates with reservation of seats at the first Round Table Conference. When the Indian Central Committee's report was published giving the Depressed Classes joint electorates with reservation for all provinces except Madras, there was no hue and cry, and when the Simon Commission report embodying electorates with reservation of seats was published there was no protest raised against it. My friend, Dr. Ambedkar, while speaking on the recommendations of this Commission, welcomed this system as an advancement in the interest of the community and raised objection to the system of panel from which the Governor was to select candidates for Depressed Classes. Indeed, Dr. Ambedkar speaking at Kamptee conference in 1930 declared, "No share of political powers can come to you so long as the British Government remains where it is. It is only in a Swaraj constitution that you stand any chance of getting political power in your hands." He said in the same speech, "Swaraj is going to be a system of government in which you (Depressed Classes) stand a chance, other things being equal, of being amongst those who will be installed as political sovereigns of this country."

I do not know what brought about the revolution in the state of mind of Dr. Ambedkar and Mr. Srinivasan at the second Round Table Conference when they sacrificed the system whereby they would have obtained the right to be political sovereigns, and secured instead the expression of minimum voice for the people who deserved the maximum electoral power to direct the government from within. Now, sir, it will be clear to the House that joint electorates were acceptable to my community from the time they understood that there was to be a transfer of power to Indian hands. The position we took was that under the scheme of government in which Indians would rule, our safety lay not in finding channels for voicing our opinions, but in taking our due share in the governing of the country. Indeed this is my chief attack on the Premier's letter to Mahatma Gandhi. He tells us that he has given separate electorates for twenty years to enable us to get the minimum number of seats to place our views before the Government and legislature of the day. I contend that this privilege we have already enjoyed under the Montford reforms which have enabled us to get representation in numerous local bodies and in legislatures both provincial and central. We are sufficiently organized for that purpose and. do not need either special pleading or special succour. In future what we do need as real remedy for our uplift is definite power to elect our representatives from the general constituencies and hold them responsible to us for their actions. I do not know why the Prime Minister calls the scheme of joint electorates with reservation of seats as impracticable. It is already in force in local bodies in Madras and some other provinces and has worked very satisfactorily. I contend, sir, that the scheme enunciated in the communal decision involves our segregation and makes us politically untouchables. I am surprised at the argument of the Prime Minister that there is no segregation because we can vote for Caste Hindus who will have to solicit our votes. But, sir, how can we bring about a common ideal of citizenship when Depressed Class representatives are not to solicit votes of higher castes?

There is, sir, another tragic controversy. When we claim special protection from Government for some share in official services which is given by the Government of India to other minorities and backward classes, we are told that we are classed as Hindus and have no special claim, and when we declare that in the matter of legislative representation we would like to join the general body of Hindus, we are told that we are a separate community. The sufferings which my community has undergone at the hands of Caste Hindus have been acknowledged by Caste Hindus themselves, and I am prepared to admit that there are a large number of reformers among them who are doing everything possible to improve our status and position. I am convinced that there is a change of heart and a change in the angle of vision of Caste Hindus. We, Depressed Classes, feel ourselves as true Hindus as any Caste Hindu can be, and we feel that the moral conscience of the Hindus has been roused to the extent that our salvation lies in bringing about a change from within the main body of Hindu society and not segregating ourselves from them. The course adopted by the Government would certainly arrest the progress of this most laudable movement. I must say, sir, that the Prime Minister's letter in its entire conception and expression has disappointed me. He argues, for distance, that reservation of seats under joint electorates would not be genuine representation for us. Does the Prime Minister know that the Simon Commission, consisting of seven chosen Britishers, held after a most thorough investigation on the spot that such system would produce genuine representation for us? Even the fear expressed by the Prime Minister is resolved by Mahatma Gandhi, who has said that he is ready to enroll every adult member of the Depressed Class as a voter and impose stricter test on Caste Hindus. May I ask why the Premier is not prepared to consider this solution?

Now let me summarize the position. The Premier's award of separate electorates is solely to secure a minimum number of spokesmen for the Depressed Classes. Mahatma Gandhi's decision is for over-representation of the Depressed Classes. In joint electorate my pact with Dr. Moonje of the Hindu Mahasabha gives my community reservation of seats on a population basis. In conclusion, let me add that I have known and studied the question of the Depressed Classes in all its bearings all over India, during the quarter of a century of my public life. I was privileged to review it fully during our tour with the Simon Commission. I would, therefore, ask the Government to take this assurance from me that our best interests require that we should not be dissected from the Hindu community but that we should have our due representation in legislatures on the basis of reservation. The crisis that faces us today is very grave. There hangs in the balance the life of the greatest Indian of our time, and there hangs in the balance the future of millions of the down-trodden people of this country. Is Government going to take the responsibility for killing the one and reducing the other to perpetual servitude? Let it make its choice well and wisely (Pyarelal 1932: 248-253).

**

55. Gandhi's letter to P. N. Rajbhoj

September 20, 1932

Dear Friend,

I got your letter only yesterday whilst I was talking to the friends who came to see me. I am now replying to it at the earliest opportunity. I thank you for your letter.

My position is this: My fast has reference only to separate electorate. As soon as that is withdrawn the letter of the vow will be satisfied and I would be bound to call off the fast. But a very heavy responsibility will then lie upon me of having a substitute that is infinitely superior to separate electorate.

If you will not resent my saying it, I would like to say that I as I am a "touchable" by birth, I am an "untouchable" by choice. And it was in this dual capacity that I wrote to Sir Samuel Hoare and then the Prime Minister. It is that dual capacity that has compelled the fast. Looking at the matter in this light I must say that I am not in love with the idea of statutory reservation. Whilst it is not open to the same objection that separate electorate is, I have not a shadow of a doubt that it will prevent the natural growth of the suppressed classes and will remove the incentive to honourable amends from the suppressors. What I am aiming at is a heart understanding between the two, the greatest opportunity of repentance and reparation on the part of the suppressors. I am certain that the moment is ripe for the change of heart among them. I would therefore favour widest possible franchise for the suppressed and establish a convention between the two sections for securing proper election of representatives of the suppressed. I have drafted a rough tentative scheme which I handed to the friends and which I explained fully yesterday to my son Devdas. But to me this is not the largest but it is the least part of the reform I want.

Nothing will satisfy me till the last vestige of untouchability is gone. I would therefore insist on a statutory declaration that all public places of worship, wells, schools, etc., should be open to the suppressed precisely on the same terms as the suppressors. This is roughly my idea. If, however, the representatives of suppressed classes will not look at my idea, they are at liberty to have statutory reservation of seats. I should not fast against it but you will not expect me to bless any such scheme. Nor is my blessing essential to its acceptance by the Government. If I get the opportunity, I should certainly try to create public opinion among the suppressed against statutory reservation.

If my position is not clear or satisfactory, I would be delighted to meet you and other friends including R. B. Rajah and Dr. Ambedkar by appointment. As you are aware this has become possible only now.

Yours sincerely,

M. K. GANDHI

(Gandhi 1972 LI: 111-112).

Section V
Pacts and Awards

56. Minorities Pact

Second Round Table Conference

Provisions for a Settlement of the Communal Problem, put forward jointly by Muslims, Depressed Classes, Indian Christians, Anglo-Indians and Europeans.

Claims of Minority Communities

1. No person shall by reason of his origin, religion, caste or creed, be prejudiced in any way in regard to public employment of his civic rights and the exercise of any trade or calling.
2. Statutory safeguards shall be incorporated in the constitution with a view to protect against enactments of the Legislature of discriminatory laws affecting any community.
3. Full religious liberty, that is, full liberty of belief, worship observances, propaganda, associations and education, shall be guaranteed to all communities subject to the maintenance of public order and morality.

   No person shall merely by change of faith lose any civic right or privilege, or be subject to any penalty.
4. The right to establish, manage and control at their own expense, charitable, religious and social institutions, schools and other educational establishments with the right to exercise their religion there in.
5. The constitution shall embody adequate safeguards for the protection of religion, culture and personal law, and the promotion of education, Language, charitable institutions of the minority communities and for their due share in grants-in-aid given by the State by the self-governing bodies.
6. Enjoyment of civic rights by all citizens shall be guaranteed by making any act or omission calculated to prevent full enjoyment an office punishable by law.
7. In the formation of Cabinets in the Central Government and provincial Governments, so far as possible, members belonging to the Mussalman community and other minorities of considerable number shall be included by convention.
8. There shall be Statutory Departments under the Central and provincial Governors to protect minority communities and to promote their welfare.
9. All communities at present enjoying representation in any Legislature through nomination or election shall have representation in all Legislatures through separate electorates and the minorities shall have

not less than the proportion set forth in Annexure but no majority shall be reduced to a minority or even an equality. Provided that after a lapse of ten years it will be open to Muslims in Punjab and Bengal and any minority communities in any other Provinces to accept joint electorates, or joint electorates with reservation of seats, by the consent of the community concerned. Similarly after the lapse of ten years, it will be open to any minority in the Central Legislature to accept joint electorates with or without reservation of seats with the consent of the community concerned.

With regard to the Depressed Classes, no change to joint electorates and reserved seats shall be made until after 20 years experience of separate electorates and until direct adult suffrage for the community has been established.

10. In every province and in connection with the Central Government, a public Services Commission shall be appointed, and the recruitment to the public Services, except the proportion, if any reserved to be filled by nomination by the Governor-General and the Governors, shall be made through such commission in such a way as to secure a fair representation to the various communities consistently with the considerations of efficiency and the possession of the necessary qualifications. Instructions to the Governor-General and the Governors in the Instrument of Instructions with regard to recruitment shall be embodied to give effect to this principle, and for that purpose to review periodically the composition of the Service.

11. If a Bill is passed which, in the opinion of two-thirds of the members of any Legislature representing a particular community, affects their religion or social practice based on religion, or in the case of fundamental rights of the subjects if one-third of the members object, it shall be open to such members to lodge their objection thereto, within a period of one month of the Bill being passed by the House, with the President of the House who shall forward the same to the Governor-General or the Governor, as the case may be, and he shall thereupon suspend the operation of that Bill for one year, upon the expiry of which period he shall remit the said Bill for further consideration by the Legislature. When such Bill has been further considered by the Legislature and the Legislature concerned has refused to revise or modify the Bill so as to meet the objection thereto the Governor-General, as the case may be, may give or withhold his assent to it in the exercise of his assent to it in the exercise of his discretion, provided, further that the validity of such Bill may be challenged in the Supreme Court by any two members of the denomination affected thereby on the ground that it contravenes one of their fundamental rights.

Special Claims of Mussulman

A — The North-West Frontier Province shall be constituted a Governor's Province on the same footing as other Provinces with due regard to the necessary requirements for the security of the Frontier.

In the formation of the Provincial Legislature, the nomination shall not exceed more than 10 per cent of the whole.

B — Sind shall be separated from the Bombay Presidency and made a Governor's Province similar to and on the same footing as other Provinces in British India.

C—Mussulman representation in the Central Legislature shall be one-third of the total number of the House, and their representation in the Central Legislature shall not be less than the proportion set forth in the Annexure.

Special claims of the Depressed Classes

A—The constitution shall declare invalid any custom or usage by which any penalty or disadvantage or disability is imposed upon or any discrimination is made against any subject of the State in regard to the enjoyment of the civic rights on account of Untouchability.

B—Generous treatment in the matter of recruitment to Public Services and the opening of enlistment in the Police and Military Services.

C—The Depressed Classes in the Punjab shall have the benefit of the Punjab Land Alienation Act extended to them.

D—Right of Appeal shall lie to the Governor or Governor-General for redress of prejudicial action or neglect of interest by any Executive Authority.

E—The Depressed Classes shall have representation not less than set forth in the Annexure.

Special Claims of the Anglo-Indian community

A—Generous interpretation of the claims admitted by Sub-Committee No.VIII (Services) to the effect that in recognition of the peculiar position of the community, special consideration should be given to the claim for public employment, having regard to the maintenance of an adequate standard of living.

B—The right to administer and control its own educational institutions, i.e. European education, subject to the control of the Minister.

Provisions for generous and adequate grants-in-aid and scholarship on the basis of present grants.

C—Jury rights equal to those enjoyed by other communities in India unconditionally of proof of legitimacy and descent and the right of accused persons to claim trial by either a European or an Indian Jury.

Special Claims of the European Community

A—Equal rights and privileges to those enjoyed by Indian born subjects in all industrial and commercial activities.

B—The maintenance of existing rights in regard to procedure of criminal trials, and any measure or bill to amend, alter, or modify such a procedure cannot be introduced except with the previous consent of the Governor General.

Agreed by:

His Highness the Aga Khan (Muslims)

Dr. Ambedkar (Depressed Classes)

Rao Bahadur Pannir Selvam (Indian Christians)

Sir Henry Gidney (Anglo-Indians)

Sir Hubert Carr (Europeans)

Annexure

REPRESENTATION IN LEGISLATURES

Figures in bracket – population basis 1931 figures and depressed percentages as per Simon Report

Center	Strength Of Chambers	Caste	Hindu Depressed	Total	Musl	Chris	Sikhs	Anglo Indian	Tribal etc	Euro -peans	Remarks
All India	200	(47.5)	(19)*	(66.5)	(21.5)	1	6	1	–	4	*Represents
(1931) Upper		101	20	121	67						percentage in
Lower	300	123	45	168	100	7	10	3	–	12	Governor's
Assam	*100	(48.9)	(13.4)	(62.3)	(34.8)	3	–	1	–	10	Provinces of B.I.
		38	13	51	35						*Pop. Figures
Bengal	200	(18.3)	(24.7)	(43)	(54.9)	2	–	3	–	20	exclude Tribal
		38	35	73	102						Areas
Bihar and		100	(67.8)	(14.5)	(82.3)	(11.3)	1	–	1	3	5*On Sind being
Orissa		51	14	65	25						separated Weight
Bombay	200	(68)	(8)	(76)	(20)	2	–	3	–	13	age to Mussu lmans In Bombay
		88	28	116	66						
C.P.	100	(63.1)	(23.7)	(86.8)	(44)	1	–	2	2	2	to be on the same
		58	20	78	15						footing as to
Madras	200	(71.3)	(15.4)	(86.7)	(7.1)	(3.7)	–	4	2	8	Hindus in the
		102	40	142	30	14					N.W.F.P
Punjab	100	(15.1)	(13.5)	(28.6)	(56.5)	1.5	(13)	(1.5)	–	2	
U.P.	100	(58.1)	(26.4)	(84.5)	(14.8)	1	–	2	–	3	
		44	20	64	30						

Sind and N.W.F.P. Weightage similar to that enjoyed by the Mussulamans in Provinces in which they constitute a minority of the population, shall be given to the Hindu minority in Sind and to the Hindu and Sikh minorities in the N.W.F.P.

(Ambedkar 1991 vol IX: 307-311).

57. British Prime Minister's Communal Award

17 August 1932

(The section pertaining to the Untouchables is reproduced below)

In the statement made by the Prime Minister on 1st December last on behalf of His Majesty's Government at the close of the second session of the Round Table Conference, which was immediately afterwards endorsed by both Houses of Parliament, it was made plain that if the communities in India were unable to reach a settlement acceptable to all parties on the communal questions which the Conference had failed to solve, His Majesty's Government were determined that India's constitutional advance should not on that account be frustrated, and that they would remove this obstacle by devising and applying themselves a provisional scheme.

2. On the 19th March last His Majesty's Government, having been informed that the continued failure of the communities to reach agreement was blocking the progress of the plans for the framing of a new Constitution, stated that they were engaged upon a careful re-examination of the difficult and controversial questions which arise. They are now satisfied that without a decision of at least some aspects of the problems connected with the position of minorities under the new Constitution, no further progress can be made with the framing of the Constitution.

3. His Majesty's Government have accordingly decided that they will include provisions to give effect to the scheme set out below in the proposals relating to the Indian Constitution to be laid in due course before Parliament. The scope of this scheme is purposely confined to the arrangements to be made for the representation of the British Indian communities in the Provincial Legislatures, consideration of representation in the Legislature at the Center being deferred for the reason given in paragraph 20 below. The decision to limit the scope of the scheme implies no failure to realize that the framing of the Constitution will necessitate the decision of a number of other problems of great importance to minorities, but has been taken in the hope that once a pronouncement has been made upon the basic questions of method and proportions of representation the communities themselves may find it possible to arrive at *modus vivendi* on other communal problems, which have not received the examination they require.

4. His Majesty's Government wish it to be most clearly understood that they themselves can be no parties to any negotiations which may be initiated with a view to the revision of their decision, and will not be prepared to give consideration to any representation aimed at securing

the modification of it which is not supported by all the parties affected. But they are most desirous to close no door to an agreed settlement should such happily be forthcoming. If, therefore, before a new Government of India Act has passed into law, they are satisfied that the communities who are concerned are mutually agreed upon a practicable alternative scheme, either in respect of any one or more of the Governors' Provinces or in respect of the whole of the British India, they will be prepared to recommend to Parliament that alternative should be substituted for the provisions now outlined.

5. * * * *

6. * * * *

7. * * * *

8. * * * *

9. Members of the 'depressed classes' qualified to vote will vote in a general constituency. In view of the fact that for a considerable period these classes would be unlikely, by this means alone, to secure any adequate representation in the Legislature, a number of special seats will be assigned to them as shown in the table. These seats will be filled by election from special constituencies in which only members of the 'depressed classes' electorally qualified will be entitled to vote. Any person voting in such a special constituency will, as stated above, be also entitled to vote in a general constituency. It is intended that these constituencies should be formed in selected areas where the depressed classes are most numerous, and that, except in Madras, they should not cover the whole area of the Province.

In Bengal it seems possible that in some general constituencies a majority of the voters will belong to the Depressed Classes. Accordingly, pending further investigation, no number has been fixed for the members to be returned from the special Depressed Class constituencies in that Province. It is intended to secure that the Depressed Classes should obtain not less than 10 seats in the Bengal Legislature.

The precise definition in each Province of those who (if electorally qualified) will be entitled to vote in the special Depressed Class constituencies has not yet been finally determined. It will be based as a rule on the general principles advocated in the Franchise Committee's Report. Modification may, however, be found necessary in some Provinces in Northern India where the application of the general criteria of untouchability might result in a definition unsuitable in some respects to the special condition of the Province.

His Majesty's Government do not consider that these special Depressed Classed constituencies will be required for more than limited time. They intend that the Constitution shall provide that they shall come to an end after 20 years if they have not previously been abolished under the general powers of electoral revision referred to in paragraph 6 (Ambedkar 1991 vol IX: 80-82).

**

58. The Poona Pact

24 September 1932

1. There shall be seats reserved for the Depressed Classes out of general electorates. Seats in, Provincial Legislatures shall be as follows:

MADRAS			30
BOMBA Y WITH SIND	....	....	15
PUNJAB	....	....	8
BEHAR AND ORISSA	....	....	18
CENTRAL PROVINCES	....	....	20
ASSAM	....	....	7
BENGAL	....	....	30
UNITED PROVINCES	....	....	20
Total	....	....	148

These figures are based on the total strength of the Provincial Councils announced in the Prime Minister's decision.

2. Election to these seats shall be by joint electorates subject, however, to the following procedure:

All members of the Depressed Classes registered in the general electoral roll of a constituency, will form an electoral college which will elect a panel of four candidates belonging to the Depressed Classes, for each of such reserved seats by the method of single vote and four persons getting the highest number of votes in such primary election shall be the candidates for election by the general electorate.

3. Representation of the Depressed Classes in the Central Legislature shall likewise be on the principle of joint electorates and reserved seats by the method of primary election in the manner provided for in clause 2 above for their representation in Provincial Legislatures.

4. In the Central Legislature 18 per cent of the seats allotted to the general electorate for British India in the said legislature shall be reserved for the Depressed Classes.

5. The system of primary election to panel of candidates for election to the Central and Provincial Legislatures, as hereinbefore mentioned, shall come to an end after the first ten years unless terminated sooner by mutual agreement under the provision of Clause 6 below.

6. The system of representation of the Depressed Classes by reserved seats in the Provincial and Central Legislatures as provided for in clauses

1 and 4 shall continue until determined by mutual agreement between the communities concerned in this settlement.

7. The franchise for the Central and Provincial Legislatures for the Depressed Classes shall be as indicated in the Lothian Committee Report.

8. There shall be no disabilities attaching to anyone on the ground of his being member of the Depressed Classes in regard to any elections to local bodies or appointment to public service.

Every endeavour shall be made to secure a fair representation of the Depressed Classes in these respects subject to such educational qualifications as may be laid down for appointment to public services.

9. In every province out of the educational grant an adequate sum shall be earmarked for providing educational facilities to members of the Depressed Classes.

MADAN MOHAN MALAVIYA	B.S.KAMAT
TEJ BAHADUR SAPRU	G. K. DEODHAR
M.R. JAYAKAR	A.V. THAKKAR
B. R. AMBEDKAR	R.K. BAKHLE
SRINIVASAN	P.G. SOLANKI
M.C. RAJAH	P. BALOO
C. V. MEHTA	GOVIND MALAVIYA
C. RAJAHGOPALACHARI	DEVADAS GANDHI
RAJENDRA PRASAD	BISWAS
G. D. BIRLA	B. N. RAJBHOJ
RAMESHWAR DAS BIRLA	GAVAI
SHANKERLAL BANKER	

The following signatures were added in Bombay at the finial sitting of the Hindu Conference on September 25:

LALLUBHAI SAMALDAS	P. KODANDARAO
HANSA MEHTA	G. K. GADGIL
K. NATARAJAHN	MANU SUBEDAR
KAMAKOTI NATARAJAHN	AVANTIKABAI GOKHLE
PURSHOTTAMDAS THAKURDAS	K. J. CHITALIA
MATHRADAS VASSANJI	RADHAKANT MALAVIYA
WALCHAND HIRACHAND	A. R. BHAT
H, N. KUNZRU	COLAM
K. G. LIMAYE	PRADHAN

(Pyarelal 1932:153-156).

**

Appendixes*

Appendix I
Memorandums and petitions

Memorial

Hail to the Government

To

His Excellency the Right Honourable Freeman Freeman-Thomas, Earl of Willingdon, G.M.S.I., G.C.M.G., G.M.I.E., G.B.E.

Viceroy and Governor General of India.

May it please your Excellency,

We the members of the Adi Dharam Mandal Punjab Jullundur City are the representatives of down trodden community comprising four Million souls in the Punjab, and seventy Million in the whole of India, who are disgracefully called the "Shudars" or untouchables. Your Excellency may be aware that we belong to an ancient race which ruled India about 5,000 years ago, prior to the invasion of India by the Aryans. These bands of outsiders from central Asia raided India, and defeated our forefathers, the latter were most ruthlessly treated, they were forcibly made to serve their foreign cruel masters in a way which spoke volumes of the barbarous mentality of the so called "Civilized" Aryans. The rest of the conquered race, who due to their self respect, refused to be enslaved, were driven away to take shelter in the jungles. The Aryans whose present descendants are called high class Hindus, have all along been treating us with the most inhuman brutality so that our unlucky community numerically large as it is, is now little more than a mere name. Inspite of the fact that there are some highly educated and capable men in our community still we are not given any honourable status in society. No right of ownership of any thing, rests in us, even we have not the right to safeguard our individual lives. This deplorable condition of the mute million of our oppressed community is due to harsh treatment meted out to us by the high class Hindus in consequence of the "August" pronouncements of the ancient Aryans which are embodied in the Manu Smriti and a lot of other Hindu scriptures of that type. Your Excellency will be amazed to learn that the scriptures of the so called religion are replete with the sayings such as that we the Adi Dharmies have been created to serve the high class Hindus, that we have no right to hold any property, that even our wanton murder by a high class Hindu involves him in no difficultly, etc. All our demands have been willfully suppressed by high class Hindus, and all our attempts at ameliorating our condition have been deliberately trampled upon. We therefore beg to submit the position and demands of our community which we venture to hope will receive adequate consideration at your hands. We are sorry to say that the Hindu officials who appropriated all our rights and privileges have not done any justice to us. All the dealings of the Government with the Hindus mean with the high class Hindus only, with the result that our grievances cannot reach the Government. It would be no exaggeration to say that the reforms given to Hindus have been so given to the high class Hindus only. This being so, we are now under two Governments, the high class Hindus Government and the present British Government.

Owing to the predominance of the Muslims there is less untouchability in this province, as compared with other provinces but as regards political condition we are not a bit better than the worst untouchables of other Provinces, but we are in the worst condition from the political point of view. Not even a single member of our community has ever been nominated to the local legislature or to any local body although in other provinces such nominations have been made by the Government to the extant of seats ranging between 1 to 11 in local legislatures. The present system of electorate cannot be of any use to us because the high class Hindus are steeped in caste prejudices. Therefore the only method open to us should be separate electorate where in our political social and even moral salvation lies.

Our position can be briefly described as follows: -

(1) That our community consist of about four Millions in the Punjab and about seventy million in whole of India

(2) That comparatively speaking we are the most backward people in the Punjab as regards education, public services, social position etc.

(3) That we do not believe in the Hindu religion, nor do we hold it in high esteem, therefore we do not wish to call ourselves Hindus but we the all untouchables of different classes being the ancient population of India wish to be called "Addharmies."

(4) We do not desire to keep any close social or political contact with the high caste Hindus, who think that they are polluted by our mere touch or even by the casting of our shadow on them though they endeavour to count us with them so that they may enjoy greater rights at our expense. So this aspect of our position can be remedied by the grant of our following petty demands.

Our Demands

1. The 'Ad Dharam' should be accepted as a separate body from the Hindu Community.
2. We, the Ad Dharamies strongly condemn the joint electorate system, and are in favour of separate electorate, in all Public bodies and legislatures. The representation to be selected by the Committee of our Mandal.

3. No change in Constitution of the Central Government should be made unless the question of representation of Minorities is settled.

4. a) Share in all Public services, including Police, Civil, Military, Railway, Education, and Medical etc. Our separate Military regiment should be established by the Ad Dharmi names.

   b) Our representation in Municipalities and District Boards, Councils, and Assembly according to our number are immediate and special demands; we urge 18% representation of our Community.

5. a) The Punjab Alienation Act has made us so weak that the people of other Communities forcibly make us to do their service in return of living in the houses built on their lands, because we cannot buy any land even for our houses under the Punjab Alienation of Land Act of 1900 A.D. Therefore provisions be made in this act for the benefit of Ad Dharmies.

   b) Equal rights of ownership of any property of dwelling houses and common fields as enjoyed by other Communities, the full ownership of the houses, where ever they are situated, and of long standing are strongly demanded.

   c) Our caste do the work of agriculture with agriculturist but they give very meagre share to the poor (untouchables) and we hear that there are 15,18,72,000 acres of un-cultivated land in the hands of the Punjab government, therefore, land in the new colonies should be reserved for us in the same way as it has been done for other Communities.

6. a) The law that we, the Ad Dharmies, are not allowed to stand as security in legal matters for another Ad-Dharmies, should be altered as it has retarded our Progress in various activities.

   b) There is criminal blame upon our Community. While we are free from every crime, therefore, this blame should be wiped off. The natural presumption of innocence should attach to Ad-Dharmies as well.

7. Permission should be given to us to go to the foreign countries, viz., Canada, New Zealand, Australia etc, as our condition is very poor.

8. The professional tax to be levied on the Ad Dharmies by the Municipalities and District Boards, is highly objectionable, we beg therefore, the abolition or suspension of the tax unless our representatives are taken into the bodies in question.

9. The Banking facilities afforded by the government to the rural population, have not, in the least benefited the un-touchables, so the special Banking arrangements are badly needed by us under the government control.

10. Either our representations should be included into the rural Panchayats, or our (of the Ad-Dharmies) separate rural Panchayats, should be legally established.

11.a) Owing to the Coercion practised by the Hindus & Sikhs against Ad-Dharmies, the census of this year is not acceptable to us, therefore a correct estimate of the Ad-Dharmies should be made after an enquiry into the alleged excesses of the Hindus and Sikhs.

b) Since the census of 1931, almost in every village where the Hindus and Sikhs are in majority, Ad-Dharmies have been very much oppressed and the attention of the authorities has been drawn to these facts. Special measure be taken for its prevention.

12 a) Necessary arrangements for better education of Ad-Dharmies (boys, and girls), and national scholarships should be separately given to them. Arrangement for separate schools should also be made as far as possible.

b) Although the Ad-Dharmi scouts have been exempted from school fees in the Primary classes (for which we are grateful to the government) yet in the middle classes it is burdensome on account of poverty and besides its exemption, we request the authorities to grant scholarships.

13.The Ad Dharam Mandal of Punjab, Jullunder City should be accepted as representing the Ad-Dharma community. Daya Nand Dalit Udhar Mandal Hoshiarpur, Patit Udhar Mandal, Achhut Udhar Mandal and Antaj Udhar Mandal Lahore are not representative of Ad Dharam community (untouchables)

14.At least one representative of Ad Dharmies nominated by the Ad Dharma Mandal Punjab Jullundur City should be sent to the round table conference to be held in London.

15.It is the earnest desire of the Ad Dharmies that the government should show a favour by buying through the Ad Dharma Mandal of Punjab Jullunder the leather articles supplied by other communities and used for the requirements of armies. Police department etc. We desire that we should no longer be deprived of the benefit of this occupation which up to this time has unfairly been received by others.

We have the honour to be

Sirs,

Your most obedient admirers

The members of Ad Dharam (Aboriginese) Mandal

(Punjab) Jullundur City.

**

Appendix II

The Madras Adi-Dravida Mahajana Sabha

(Registered Under Act XXI of 1860)

(Estd. Dec. 1892)

Madras, 15-9-31

The Madras Depressed Classes Conference.

The Conference of the Depressed Classes held under the auspices of the Madras Audi-Dravida Mahajana Sabha, assembled in the Gokhale Hall, under the Presidency of Swami Sahajanandajee, M.L.C., passed the following resolution:-

1. Representation of Depressed Classes at the R.T.C. : -

a. The Conference heartily congratulates Dr. Ambedkar and Rao Bahadur R. Sreenivasan, on their being elected as representatives of the Depressed Classes to the Round Table Conference.

b. It requests the British Government and the delegates of the R.T.C. to recognise them as the two representatives of the Depressed Classes throughout India, who constitute one-sixth of the total population.

2. Representation: -

a. It requests that, in all Local Boards, Legislative Council, Assembly and Council of State and other public bodies; one-sixth of the seats be reserved for this community in proportion to the population.

b. It considers that this reservation is essential in order that this community may attain equal status in due course with other communities who have the benefit of education and other privileges.

c. It specially urges that its representation in all public bodies should not in any way be inferior to the strength that may be given to the Muslim community.

3. Franchise and Separate Electorates: -

a. This conference, recognising its present inability to succeed in the elections, considers the reservation of seats quite essential, until the curse of untouchability is removed and the community is able to assert its individuality in an atmosphere of unrestricted freedom.

b. It requests that one-sixth of the seats in all districts may be reserved for the Depressed Classes irrespective of the total number of votes.

c. It further resolves that franchise must be extended to the members of the Depressed Classes on the qualification of their Primary Education and not on the basis of the tax-payment.

d. It requests that the qualification for the franchise be fixed as the payment of one rupee towards revenue in lieu of the minimum education.

e. In the case of Assembly and Council of State, the qualification shall be Higher Elementary Education and in the alternative, payment of two rupees towards revenue.

4. Services: -

a. In all cases of offices from Provincial Governorships to the lowest grade, a sixth of the total strength should be reserved to the Depressed Classes.

b. For the present, such services should be distributed in accordance with the experience of the individuals of this community.

c. The Government are requested to appoint the members of the Depressed Classes to all Offices in proportion to their number and necessary steps in this direction should be taken immediately.

5. Finance: -

a. This Conference requests the Government to set apart a sixth of the surplus amount at its credit for the amelioration of the Depressed Classes.

b. It further requests that the Local Boards shall also act similarly.

6. Social: -

This Conference strongly urges that all Public Schools, public wells, places of worship, etc. shall be thrown open to them and they should be given equal privileges as enjoyed by Hindu, Christian and Muslim and other communities.

7. Religion: -

a. As the Depressed Classes are classed among the Hindus, all the privileges such as temple-entry, enjoyed by the Hindu should also be conceded to them.

b. If the Depressed Classes are not granted these privileges, they may as well be classified under a different nomenclature.

c. The Conference further requests that the Depressed Classes should be granted all such privileges specially reserved to other minorities as Anglo-Indians, Muslims, etc.

8. This Conference authorises the President to communicate these resolutions to the British Government and the Round Table Conference.

**

Appendix III

INDIAN POST AND TELEGRAPHS DEPARTMENT

New Delhi, Stamp

O MD Haldwani 12 66 Dated 12 March, 1931

His Excellency the Viceroy and Governor General of India Delhi

A Mass Meeting of Shilpkar Shudharni Working Committee Kumaun Decided Dr. Ambedkar Indian Delegate Round Table Conference to lead our cases for Separate Election and seats in councils and Boards Depress Class deceived with High Class Hindoos Represent our cause to Round Table Conference

Khusi Ram President Shilpkar Shudharni
Society Kumaun Member District Board
Nainital

13/28

**

Appendix IV

INDIAN POSTS AND TELEGRAPHS DEPARTMENT

Received here at—H.—M.

(New Delhi P.O. Stamp Dated 3 Nov. 1931)

TC Hinganghat 2 34

Private secy to his excellency the viceroy Viceroys camp Depressed Class meeting held 24th October unanimously supports separate representation for Depressed Classes Expresses full confidence in Doctor Ambedkar

Amrutrai President Depressed Class Meeting.

Delhi; the 30.11.1931 Sd.

Assistant Private Secy. to the Viceroy.

**

Appendix V

OFFICE OF THE ADI HINDU (ABORIGINES) SABHA (DEPRESSED & BACKWARD CLASS) FARRUKHABAD

No..... 41 Dated 26.11.1931

His Excellency the Viceroy of India

Delhi

A meeting of depressed classes was held today the 25th November 1931 at 7 P.M. under the presidentship of Mr. Janki Prasad Dhanuk of Aliganj at Narkasa Dist., Farrukhabad. The meeting represented all the depressed classes viz., Kori, Chamar, Dhobi, Dhanuk, Kanjar, Jallad, Bahelia etc.

After Bhajans and lectures the following resolution was passed unanimously:-

1. Resolved that this meeting congratulates the rights offered to the depressed classes by the Government and prays for the long life of His Majesty the King and his government.

2. Resolved that this meeting has full confidence on Dr. Ambedkar Barrister and Sri Nivasam Rao Bahadur, the delegates to the Round Table Conference representing the depressed classes, and has no confidence in Mahatma Gandhi and the congress.

3. This meeting supports the memorandum of the All India depressed classes Conference which was held at Gurgaon district on 31st October 1931.

4. This meeting recommends the proper publication of the resolution.

Sd. Dwarka Prasad

Secretary

Adi Hindu Sabha Farrukhabad

**

Appendix VI

From:-

G.R. Pradhan. Esqr.

B.A. L. L.B. Ex, M.L.C.

Chairman Municipal Board & Vice Chairman Distt Board Nagpur.

President-Kahar Sudharak Maha Sabha

To,

His Excellency the Viceroy and Governor General of India,

Through:

The Private Secretary to His Excellency the Viceroy, New Delhi

No. 73 Dated Head Office Tribhuvan Mandir, Bhupal C.I.

May it please your Excellency,

Most submissively I have the honour to send here-with a copy of the resolution passed at the meeting of the Kahar Leaders Conference held at Hoshangabad C.P. on the 25th 26th & 27th December 1931, for information & favour of an action.

I have the honour to be,

Sir,

Your Excellency's most obedient servant,

Indirjet Singh

L.M.P. H.M.B.

General Secretary K.S.M. Sabha

for President.

Copy forwarded for information & favour of necessary action to:-

1. The Rt. Honble The Prime Minister of England 10 Downning Street Ln. Through the Private Secretary.

2. The Rt. Honble the Secretary of States for India. India House Ln. Through the Private Secretary.

3. The President, the Indian Statuary Commission, India with reference to the correspondence ending with his letter No: E.U.P.- 363 dated London the 16th, May, 1929.

Copy of the Resolution

I. Resolved that the Kahar Leaders Conference requests the Framers of the Indian Federal Constitution that the constitution in question be so framed so as to give a full and free scope to the Kahar

community in all trades & professions relating with the water ranging from the ponds and ferries to the Indian mercantile marine and the Indian Navy. In the former this community may be allowed to enjoy all the privileges freely and in the latter it may also be encouraged to represent itself on the ground that this community has been dealing with all these things from the time immemorial to the present day.

II. Resolved that the copies of the above resolution be sent to the following for information and favour of an early action:-

1. The Prime Minister of the British Cabinet.
2. The Secretary of State for India.
3. His Excellency the Viceroy.
4. The President of the Indian Statuary Commission.

The Resolution was unanimously carried.

Head Office:-
Indirjet Singh
Tribhuvan Mandir
L.M.P. H.M.B.
Bhupal, Estate, C. I.
General Secretary
India Kahar Sudharak Maha Sabha
for President

**

*Source for Appendixes N. A. I.: File 111/32-R

Biographical Sketches

Ambedkar, B.R. (1891-1956), studied at Elphinstone College, Columbia University and the London School of Economics. On return to India in 1917, he was appointed Professor of Economics at Sydenham College, Bombay. He went back to England in 1920 to complete his studies and was called to the Bar in 1923. He began his legal practice at the Bombay High Court in 1924, from when his political career commenced.

In January 1919, Ambedkar appeared before the Southborough Committee demanding political rights for the Depressed Classes. He founded the *Bahishkrit Hitkarni Sabha* in 1924 to improve the conditions of the Depressed Classes. From December 1919 to June 1920, he published a Marathi fortnightly, *Mooknayak* (Leader of the Dumb). In April 1927, he started a Marathi fortnightly, in March 1929 the paper *Samata*, and in November 1930, a weekly *Janata*.

In December 1927, Ambedkar led a *satyagraha* to demand the right of Untouchables to draw water from a public tank, the Chavdar Talen, in Mahad, District Kolaba. In March 1930, he led another movement to secure Untouchables the right to entry to the Kalaram Temple in Nasik.

Ambedkar was nominated member of the Bombay Legislative Assembly from 1926 to 1934. He was nominated delegate to the three Round Table Conferences (1930-1933). At the second Round Table Conference (November 1931), he demanded separate electorates for the Untouchables, a demand the British conceded on 17 August 1932. Gandhi announced a fast unto death against the Communal Award. Eventually the Poona Pact was signed on 24 September whereby separate electorates were rejected in favour of a joint electorate.

In July 1942, some weeks before Congress passed the Quit India resolution, Ambedkar was nominated to the Viceroy's Executive Council, of which he remained a member till 1946. He was nominated by the Congress to the Constituent Assembly and served as Law Minister in Jawaharlal Nehru's Cabinet. He was appointed Chairman of the Drafting Committee to frame India's constitution. He lost the election to Parliament in 1952 and 1953.

In 1935, at a public meeting at Yeola, Nasik, Ambedkar declared that though born a Hindu, he would not die a Hindu. He first explored the possibilities of converting to Sikhism. Finally, in October 1956, some months before his death, he embraced Buddhism.

Gawai, G.A. (1888-1973), a Mahar from Maharashtra, opposed the conversion of Depressed Classes to Christianity in his home district of Amravati. He was influenced by Vitthal Ramji Shinde and held that the Depressed Classes should fight untouchability and casteism and not embrace another religion. In 1909, he became a member of the Brahmo Samaj.

Well before Ambedkar's *Bahishkrit Hitkarni Sabha*, Gavai formed the *Mahar Sudharak Mandal* at Amravati in 1910 to create awareness among the Depressed Classes. He participated in the meeting of the Depressed Classes Mission in Bombay in November 1917 convened by Narayanrao Chandavarkar. In January 1918, he formed the Depressed India Association. He was nominated to the Central Provinces and Berar Legislative Assembly in 1920 and remained a member till 1945. He was among the founding members of the All India Depressed Classes Association in 1928 and served as its General Secretary till its dissolution in 1944. He differed with Ambedkar on the issue of separate electorates and endorsed the Rajah-Moonje Pact. He was a signatory of the Poona Pact. He became a member of the Hindu Mahasabha and remained so till his death.

Rajah, M.C. (1883-1942), of the Pariah caste, was educated at Christian College, Madras. He was nominated to the Elementary Education Committee in 1917 and to the Madras University Senate in 1924. He was appointed member of the Chinglepet District Elementary Education Committee, the Secondary Education Reorganization Committee and the Advisory Committee on Education, Madras. He started the Dravidian School at Nungambakkam in 1936. He was greatly interested in the spread of education and wrote textbooks for schools. Two works he authored were "*The Oppressed Hindus*" and "*King George*."

Rajah became Secretary of the state *Adi Dravida Mahajan Sabha* in 1916. He presided over the inaugural session of the All India Depressed Classes Association, established in 1928, and was elected its President. He was elected Vice-President of the Hindu Mahasabha and President of the Madras Temple Entry Sangam. He was the first Adi-Dravida to enter the Madras Legislative Council in 1920 and remained member till 1926.

Rajah was elected Deputy Leader of the South Indian Liberal Federation Constitutional Party. He was member of the Madras Publicity Board, Madras Soldiers' Board, Madras Labour Advisory Board, Railway Finance Committee, Standing Committee on Emigration, Advisory Committee to Simon Commission and the Indian Central Commission.

In 1927, Rajah was nominated member of Indian Legislative Assembly and remained member for a decade. In 1932, he entered into a pact with

B.S. Moonje of the Hindu Mahasabha for a joint electorate and was a signatory to the Poona Pact. He joined Ambedkar's Scheduled Castes Federation in 1942 in protest against the Cripps proposals, which were regarded inimical to the interests of the Depressed Classes.

Rajbhoj, P.N. (1905-1984), of the Chambhar community, was educated at the Maharashtra Education Society's High School, Pune. He participated in several protests led by Dr. Ambedkar, including the *satyagraha* at Mahad Choudar Tank in March 1927, the temple entry *satyagraha* at Parvati Mandir in Poona in October 1928 and the Kala Ram Mandir *satyagraha* in Nasik in 1930. In December 1931, he presided over the Poona unit meeting of the All India Depressed Classes Association which supported the Rajah-Moonje Pact. He was a signatory of the Poona Pact. In January 1936, at a meeting of the Working Committee of the All India Depressed Classes League at Lucknow, he, with Jagjivan Ram, opposed the conversion move by Dr Ambedkar. He later changed his views. He was present at the founding of the Scheduled Castes Federation in 1942 and was elected its General Secretary. He embraced Buddhism in 1957.

Rajbhoj actively participated in elections. He was a member of the Poona Municipality from 1927 to 1930 and of the Poona District Local Board from 1929 to 1932. He fought elections for the Maharashtra Legislative Assembly in 1937 as an independent from Bombay, but was defeated by Ambedkar's Independent Labour Party candidate.

Solanki, P.G. (1876-1953), was a Mahya Vanshi from Surat. He studied at the Grant Medical College, Bombay and joined the medical profession. He came into contact with Narayanrao Chandavarkar and was influenced by him. He was a member of the Depressed Classes Mission and the Servants of India Society. He converted to Christianity in 1925. He was nominated to the Bombay Legislative Council in 1927. He endorsed Ambedkar's deposition before the Simon Commission. He was a signatory of the Poona Pact. He contested the 1937 elections for the Bombay Legislative Assembly successfully. Subsequently he joined Ambedkar's Independent Labour Party, but left it in 1940.

Srinivasan, R. (1859-1945), founded the Adi-Dravida Mahajan Sabha in 1891 and organized the first conference of the Untouchables in December 1893. He worked in South Africa from 1904-1920 and it was from him that Mahatma Gandhi learnt Tamil. He was nominated member of the Madras Legislative Council in 1923 and remained member till 1935. He was nominated representative of the Depressed Classes to the Round Table Conference along with Ambedkar. He, however, did not support Ambedkar's conversion move and drifted away from him.

G M Thaware (1902-1952), a Mahar from Amravati, Maharashtra, was nominated to the Nagpur District Council in 1928-29, served as Honorary Magistrate between 1934-38 and again from 1940 to 1944. He worked as District Assistant Recruiting Officer in 1941-42. He was associated with the Hindu Mahasabha for some time. From 1928 to 1944 he was Secretary of the All India Depressed Classes Association. He joined the Scheduled Castes Federation in 1945 and remained a member till 1949.

Index